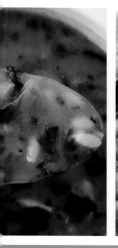

40 DAYS TO
BETTER LIVING
COOKBOOK

YOUR EASY-TO-USE GUIDE TO DELICIOUS, HEALTHFUL MEALS

The Church Health Center of Memphis, Inc.

BARBOUR
PUBLISHING

Cover and Interior Photography: Rachel Thompson Davis, Lizy Heard, and John Shorb

Published by Barbour Publishing, Inc., P.O. Box 719, Uhrichsville, Ohio 44683 www.barbourbooks.com

Our mission is to publish and distribute inspirational products offering exceptional value and biblical encouragement to the masses.

Member of the
Evangelical Christian
Publishers Association

Printed in the United States of America.

Contents

Welcome!

The *40 Days to Better Living Cookbook* was created as a user-friendly meal planning guide for healthy eating. If you've identified nutrition as an area of improvement in your life, this cookbook provides breakfasts, lunches, dinners (even snacks!) to choose from, as well as simple tips for obtaining the recommended servings of essential food groups.

Growing out of the 40 Days to Better Living series—a collection of books addressing specific health concerns such as diabetes, weight management, anxiety, and aging—this cookbook also follows the "Model for Healthy Living" as a tool to encourage overall wellness in body and spirit. The model, developed by the Church Health Center of Memphis, proposes that healthy living means that all aspects of our lives are in balance. In the words of Church Health Center founder Dr. Scott Morris, "Your faith, work, nutrition, movement, family and friends, emotions, and medical health all contribute to a life filled with more joy, more love, and more connection with God."

Nutrition, or healthy eating, is basically a diet that includes the appropriate number of servings from each of the essential food groups: water, carbohydrates, protein, and vitamins and minerals.

- **Water** is the most vital nutrient. Your body is 70 percent water—and water is needed for every process in the body. Drinking water throughout the day ensures a regular supply. Generally, drink 6 to 8 glassfuls per day.

- **Carbohydrates** are needed for energy. The best sources are whole grains, vegetables, and fruits. Too few carbohydrates can lead to hunger and tiredness—but too many can result in weight gain.

- **Protein** is used for building and repairing your body's cells. Protein-rich foods include eggs, fish, meat, nuts, seeds, and whole grains.

- **Vitamins and minerals** include many different substances. Some minerals, such as calcium, are needed in large amounts for strong bones and teeth. Vitamins are equally important but needed in minute quantities.

Another common food group is fat, and there are two basic types:

- **Essential fatty acids (EFAs)** are needed for normal function of hormones and enzymes in our bodies.

- **Saturated fats** are used as fuel by the body—or stored as fat if not burned as fuel. We should try to limit these saturated fats.

Getting the appropriate servings of each food group every day requires careful meal planning. And the *40 Days to Better Living Cookbook* provides a simple method for you and your family to enjoy a wonderful variety of healthful and delicious meals. Just follow the simple steps outlined below.

1. Determine the number of calories recommended for your age and gender.

A chart with general recommendations is provided. This is not a one-size-fits-all chart so please take lifestyle, age, and special health circumstances into account.

	Women ages 19 to 50	*Women over 50*	*Men ages 19 to 50*	*Men over 50*
Calories	1,800–2,000	1,600	2,200–2,600	2,200
Protein	46 g	46 g	56 g	56 g
Fat	40–78 g	36–62 g	49–100 g	49–85 g
Saturated fat	<20 g	<18 g	<28 g	<24 g
Carbohydrates	130 g	130 g	130 g	130 g
Fiber	25–35 g	25–35 g	25–35 g	25–35 g
Cholesterol	300 mg	300 mg	300 mg	300 mg
Iron	18 mg	8 mg	8 mg	8 mg
Sodium	2,300 mg	1,500 mg	2,300 mg	1,500 mg
Calcium	1,000 mg	1,200 mg	1,000 mg	1,200 mg

Calories are based on a sedentary individual.
Protein should be 10–30% of calories. Fat should be 20–35% of calories

2. Choose a breakfast, lunch, dinner, and snack for each day from this *40 Days to Better Living Cookbook.*

For easier planning, the recipes are divided into breakfast, lunch, dinner, and snack chapters. In each category, you'll find 50 recipes, allowing for plenty of variety over the next 40 days. You might want to purchase a small notebook and plan out your meals (and accompanying grocery lists) one or two weeks at a time.

Keys with each recipe indicate

- **Serving size and number of servings.**

- **Nutritional analyses.** These include calorie, total fat, saturated fat, sodium, carbohydrate, fiber, and protein measurements.

- **A simple cost guide.** Since grocery prices have been very volatile in recent years, this cost guide provides a relative scale ranging from least expensive ($) to most expensive ($$$$).

- **Whether or not the meal is freezable.** An asterisk (*) indicates the dish may be frozen for up to three months.

With this information, you can choose breakfasts, lunches, dinners, and snacks to meet your individual and family tastes, nutritional needs, and budgets.

Finally, remember that mealtimes are wonderful opportunities to connect with family and friends. So throughout the book, we have included blessings that can be used at home, church suppers, or other gatherings. Starting a meal with a blessing reminds us of the many blessings we have received from God—our bodies being among them. If we treat our bodies as a blessing, nourishing them with the proper foods in the proper amounts, we will feel more satisfied, more energized, maybe a few pounds lighter—perhaps even closer to the God who made us.

That's what the *40 Days to Better Living Cookbook* is all about.

Breakfast Recipes

Almond Soy Date Shake

Prep time: 5 minutes / Makes: 4 shakes / Serving size: 1 shake

What you'll need

½ cup hot water

⅓ cup pitted dates

2 cups almond milk

1 cup vanilla soy yogurt

1 large banana, frozen

½ teaspoon vanilla

6 ice cubes

¼ teaspoon ground cinnamon

What to do

1. Place water and dates in small bowl; soak dates for 10 minutes, drain, and place in blender with remaining ingredients.

2. Blend all ingredients.

3. Serve in 4 tall glasses.

Nutrition facts
(per serving)

Calories: 120

Total fat: 1 gram

Saturated fat: 0 grams

Sodium: 41 mg

Carbohydrate: 26 grams

Fiber: 3 grams

Protein: 2 grams

Cost: $

Apple Cinnamon Bran Muffins

Prep time: 10 minutes / Cook time: 20 minutes / Makes: 12 muffins / Serving size: 1 muffin

What you'll need

1 cup white whole wheat flour

1½ teaspoons baking soda

¼ teaspoon salt

1 teaspoon ground cinnamon

1½ cups skim milk

½ cup molasses

1 egg, beaten

2 tablespoons canola oil

2 cups bran flakes cereal

2 tablespoons ground flaxseeds

½ cup grated Granny Smith apples

½ cup raisins

What to do

1. Preheat oven to 375 degrees. Coat muffin tin with canola or olive oil cooking spray (enough for 12).

2. In medium mixing bowl, sift flour, baking soda, salt, and cinnamon.

3. In another medium mixing bowl, mix milk, molasses, egg, and oil. Mix in bran cereal and flaxseeds. Stir in flour mixture, grated apples, and raisins just until ingredients are moistened. Do not overmix or muffins will be tough.

4. Evenly distribute muffins into muffin tin.

5. Bake for 20 minutes in preheated oven.

Nutrition facts
(per serving)

Calories: 146

Total fat: 3 grams

Saturated fat: 2 grams

Sodium: 266 mg

Carbohydrate: 29 grams

Fiber: 2.5 grams

Protein: 3 grams

Cost: $

*****

Cinnamon Roll Pancakes

Prep time: 10 minutes / Cook time: 20 minutes / Makes: 4 servings / Serving size: 1 pancake

What you'll need

Filling:
2 cups all natural applesauce
1 teaspoon cinnamon
½ teaspoon ground ginger

Pancakes:
¾ cup flour
¼ cup whole wheat flour
2 teaspoons baking powder
½ teaspoon cinnamon
¼ teaspoon salt
1 egg, lightly beaten

1 teaspoon vegetable oil
1 cup low-fat milk

Topping:
½ cup low-fat vanilla yogurt
½ cup toasted pecans

What to do

1. Preheat griddle to 350 degrees (or heat heavy sauté pan over medium high).
2. Lightly grease surface with cooking spray.
3. Mix applesauce, cinnamon, and ginger using whisk or fork to make sure all ingredients are well mixed; set aside.
4. Sift flours, baking powder, cinnamon, and salt; set aside.
5. Beat egg with oil and milk and stir into flour mixture to make slightly lumpy mixture.
6. Scoop onto hot griddle using ½-cup measuring cup.
7. When bubbles appear and batter begins to dry around outside ring of pancakes, flip pancake and cook for an additional 3 minutes or until well browned and done in center.
8. Place pancakes onto plate and spread each cake with 2 tablespoons of spiced applesauce.
9. Roll pancake up, making sure to keep roll tight enough to hold its shape but not so tight that applesauce squeezes out of pancake.
10. Slice roll lengthwise into 1-inch segments and place up side up.
11. Drizzle with yogurt and crumble pecans over top.

Nutrition facts (per serving)

Calories: 339 / Total fat: 13 grams / Saturated fat: 2 grams / Sodium: 397 mg
Carbohydrate: 48 grams / Fiber: 5 grams / Protein: 10 grams / Cost: $

Apple Surprise Bread

Prep time: 10 minutes / Cook time: 60 minutes / Makes: 16 slices / Serving size: 1 slice

What you'll need

1 stick light butter

¼ cup spoonable sugar substitute

¼ cup dark brown sugar

1 egg plus 2 egg whites, beaten

1 cup applesauce

½ teaspoon orange extract

½ teaspoon vanilla

1 cup flour

1 cup whole wheat flour

1 teaspoon baking powder

1 teaspoon baking soda

½ teaspoon salt

1 teaspoon ground cinnamon

½ teaspoon allspice

1 cup raisins

½ cup walnuts, chopped

8 ounces low-fat cream cheese, softened

1 teaspoon brown sugar

1 teaspoon flour

1 teaspoon orange extract

What to do

1. Preheat oven to 350 degrees. Coat loaf pan with cooking spray; set aside.

2. Blend butter, sugar substitute, and brown sugar until smooth. Stir in eggs, applesauce, orange extract, and vanilla; set aside.

3. Combine flours, baking powder, baking soda, salt, cinnamon, and allspice. Add flour mixture to butter mixture. Stir in raisins and walnuts; set aside.

4. In separate bowl, blend cream cheese, brown sugar, flour, and orange extract.

5. Pour half of bread batter into prepared pan. Spoon cream mixture on top.

6. Cover with remaining bread batter.

7. Bake for 60 minutes or until toothpick comes out clean, cool on wire rack.

Nutrition facts (per serving)

Calories: 206 / Total fat: 6 grams / Saturated fat: 2 grams / Sodium: 263 mg
Carbohydrate: 33 grams / Fiber: 3 grams / Protein: 6 grams / Cost: $

Bacon and Cheese Mini Quiche Muffins

Prep time: 10 minutes / Cook time: 20 minutes / Makes: 12 mini muffins / Serving size: 3 mini muffins

What you'll need

1 teaspoon olive oil

½ medium onion

2 eggs

½ cup pancake mix

2 strips of applewood smoked bacon, cooked and crumbled

1 teaspoon garlic powder

1 teaspoon onion powder

¼ teaspoon black pepper

2 cups baby spinach leaves

¾ cup 2% cheddar cheese

What to do

1. Preheat oven to 350 degrees. Grease mini-muffin pan with cooking spray.

2. Warm medium skillet to medium-high heat. Add olive oil and diced onions and sauté for 2 minutes. Remove from heat and allow onions to cool.

3. In medium bowl, beat eggs. Add onions and crumbled bacon and mix until combined. Stir in pancake mix and spices. Add spinach and almost all cheese (save 1 tablespoon for topping). Mix ingredients until evenly combined.

4. Spoon mixture evenly into 12 muffin cups. Top each with pinch of remaining cheese.

5. Bake for 10 minutes.

Nutrition facts
(per serving)

Calories: 170

Total fat: 7 grams

Saturated fat: 2 grams

Sodium: 445 mg

Carbohydrate: 15 grams

Fiber: 2 grams

Protein: 12 grams

Cost: $

*

Bacon and Pear Panini

Prep time: 5 minutes / Cook time: 4 minutes / Makes: 4 sandwiches / Serving size: 1 sandwich

What you'll need

4 tablespoons fig jam
8 slices whole wheat bread
2 small pears, finely sliced

4 slices reduced-sodium
    turkey bacon, cooked
2 cups baby spinach

4 (1 ounce) slices cheddar
    cheese, low-fat

What to do

1. Coat grill, skillet, or panini maker with cooking spray. Heat to medium-high temperature.

2. Spread ½ tablespoon of jam on 2 slices of bread. Layer with cheese, 1 slice turkey bacon, pear slices, and ½ cup baby spinach.

3. Place on grill and cook for 2 to 4 minutes or until cheese melts.

4. Repeat for remaining three sandwiches.

Nutrition facts (per serving)

Calories: 347 / Total fat: 8 grams / Saturated fat: 3 grams / Sodium: 564 mg
Carbohydrate: 52 grams / Fiber: 7.5 grams / Protein: 19 grams / Cost: $$

Father, thank You for this day and this food.

Keep us ever mindful of the needs of others, and help us to

be the best that we can be. In Christ's name, amen.

Banana Bread

Prep time: 10 minutes / Cook time: 35 minutes / Makes: 12 slices / Serving size: 1 slice

What you'll need

⅓ cup nonfat vanilla yogurt plus 1 tablespoon

2 cups mashed banana

3 large eggs

¼ cup canola oil

1½ cups whole wheat flour

1 cup flour

½ cup sugar

¼ cup dark brown sugar

1 tablespoon baking powder

1 tablespoon pumpkin pie spice

Dash salt

¼ teaspoon cinnamon

½ cup golden raisins, chopped

¼ cup walnuts, finely chopped

What to do

1. Preheat oven to 350 degrees

2. Coat large loaf pan with cooking spray; set aside.

3. Blend yogurt, banana, eggs, and oil in large bowl. Add all dry ingredients. Stir in raisins and walnuts.

4. Stir until blended. Spread batter into prepared pan. Bake for 35 minutes or until cake springs back when lightly touched.

5. Let cool.

Nutrition facts
(per serving)

Calories: 342

Total fat: 13 grams

Saturated fat: 3 grams

Sodium: 183 mg

Carbohydrate: 48 grams

Fiber: 4 grams

Protein: 12 grams

Cost: $

*

Banana Bread Oatmeal

Prep time: 5 minutes / Cook time: 10 minutes / Makes: 4 servings / Serving size: 1 cup oatmeal and toppings (sliced bananas, mini-chips, and brown sugar)

What you'll need

2 cups nonfat milk

2 overripe bananas, mashed

1 teaspoon vanilla

1 teaspoon cinnamon

¼ teaspoon nutmeg

¼ teaspoon salt

1 cup quick oats

2 tablespoons flaxseed

¼ cup brown sugar

1 ripe banana, sliced for topping

4 teaspoons mini chocolate chips

What to do

1. In large saucepan, whisk together milk, mashed bananas, vanilla, and spices.

2. Warm mixture over medium heat. When it starts to boil, add rolled oats and flaxseed. Cook for 5 minutes, stir occasionally.

3. Remove from heat and place ¾-cup servings into 4 bowls; top each serving with 1 tablespoon brown sugar, banana slices, and 1 teaspoon mini chocolate chips.

Nutrition facts (per serving)

Calories: 409 / Total fat: 10 grams / Saturated fat: 5 grams / Sodium: 271 mg
Carbohydrate: 71 grams / Fiber: 6 grams / Protein: 11 grams / Cost: $

Banana Nut Pancakes

Prep time: 10 minutes / Cook time: 6 minutes / Makes: 18 pancakes / Serving size: 1 pancake

What you'll need

2 cups white whole wheat flour

1 tablespoon baking soda

1 tablespoon spoonable sugar substitute

10 ounces fat-free vanilla yogurt

1 large ripe banana, mashed

¼ cup walnuts, chopped

½ cup skim milk

1 tablespoon canola oil

1 teaspoon pure vanilla

4 egg whites, beaten with an electric mixer until stiff peaks form

What to do

1. Sift flour, baking soda, and sugar substitute in large bowl. Stir well.

2. Add yogurt, banana, walnuts, milk, oil, and vanilla. Stir until all ingredients are blended; do not overmix or your pancakes will be tough.

3. Fold in egg whites.

4. Coat large, nonstick skillet to medium-high heat.

5. Ladle mixture onto hot skillet making 4-inch pancakes. Cook until edges are golden and bubbles rise to top of pancakes, flip and cook other side until golden brown, about 3 minutes on each side.

6. Continue this process with rest of batter.

7. Serve with warm maple syrup if desired.

Nutrition facts
(per serving)

Calories: 90

Total fat: 2 grams

Saturated fat: 0 grams

Sodium: 228 mg

Carbohydrate: 15 grams

Fiber: 1 gram

Protein: 3 grams

Cost: $

*

Berry Strata

Prep time: 10 minutes / Chill time: 4 hours / Cook time: 40 minutes / Makes: 6 servings / Serving size: ⅙ strata

What you'll need

2 tablespoons light butter

3 tablespoons honey

2 eggs

4 egg whites

½ cup reduced-fat ricotta cheese

3 tablespoons sugar

1 cup skim milk

1 tablespoon orange zest

¼ cup freshly squeezed orange juice

6 slices bread, torn into 1-inch pieces

10 ounces frozen or fresh mixed berries (if using frozen, thaw and drain berries)

What to do

1. Melt butter in small saucepan over low heat. Add honey and stir well; set aside.

2. In large bowl, combine eggs, egg whites, ricotta cheese, and sugar. Stir well with whisk. Add milk, zest, orange juice, butter mixture, and bread. Stir well.

3. Stir in berries.

4. Place mixture in 2-quart glass baking dish coated with cooking spray. Cover with plastic wrap and chill for at least 4 hours.

5. Preheat oven to 350 degrees. Bake for 40 minutes or until golden on top.

Nutrition facts
(per serving)

Calories: 246

Total fat: 5 grams

Saturated fat: 2 grams

Sodium: 253 mg

Carbohydrate: 38 grams

Fiber: 4 grams

Protein: 13 grams

Cost: $

Blackberry Muffins

Prep time: 10 minutes / Cook time: 18 minutes / Makes: 10 muffins / Serving size: 1 muffin

What you'll need

1 cup flour

1 cup whole wheat flour

2 tablespoons baking powder

¼ teaspoon salt

½ cup light butter, soft

1 cup spoonable sugar
   substitute

½ cup honey

2 eggs, large

1 teaspoon vanilla

½ cup fat-free milk

1 cup blackberries, fresh or
   frozen

What to do

1. Preheat oven to 350 degrees.

2. Sift flours, baking powder, and salt; set aside.

3. Beat butter, sugar, and honey.

4. Add eggs one at a time and blend well. Stir in vanilla.

5. Alternately stir in flour mixture and milk.

6. Fold in berries.

7. Spoon batter into muffin pans and bake until golden brown, about 18 minutes.

8. Cool on wire rack.

Nutrition facts (per serving)

Calories: 288 / Total fat: 7 grams / Saturated fat: 4 grams / Sodium: 289 mg
Carbohydrate: 55 grams / Fiber: 3 grams / Protein: 5 grams / Cost:$ / *

Blended Mocha Freeze

Prep time: 5 minutes / Makes: 2 mocha freezes / Serving size: 1 mocha freeze

What you'll need

1 cup very strong coffee, cold

1 tablespoon sugar

2 tablespoons spoonable sugar substitute

1 cup fat-free milk

2 cups ice

2 tablespoons chocolate syrup, light

2 tablespoons fat-free whipped topping

What to do

1. Combine all ingredients except whipped topping into blender.
2. Blend on high speed until drink is very smooth.
3. Pour into 2 glasses and top with whipped topping.

Nutrition facts (per serving)

Calories: 93 / Total fat: 0 grams / Saturated fat: 0 grams / Sodium: 84 mg
Carbohydrate: 18 grams / Fiber: 0 grams / Protein: 5 grams / Cost: $

Lord, we are thankful for the food before us; may we use it to nourish

our bodies to be in Your service. In Christ's name, amen.

Blueberry Banana Muffins

Prep time: 10 minutes / Cook time: 15 minutes / Makes: 12 muffins / Serving size: 1 muffin

What you'll need

¼ cup spoonable sugar substitute

¼ cup sugar

1½ cups whole wheat flour

2 teaspoons baking powder

1 teaspoon baking soda

1 teaspoon cinnamon

½ cup reduced-calorie orange juice

¼ cup vanilla low-fat yogurt

1 tablespoon canola oil

1 egg

1 ripe banana, mashed

¼ cup walnuts, chopped

¼ cup granola cereal, chopped

1 cup fresh or frozen blueberries

What to do

1. Preheat oven to 375 degrees.
2. Coat 12-cup muffin pan with cooking spray.
3. Combine sugar substitute, sugar, flour, baking powder, baking soda, and cinnamon in large mixing bowl; set aside.
4. Combine orange juice, yogurt, canola oil, and egg in small mixing bowl.
5. Add orange juice mixture and mashed banana to dry ingredients and stir just until all ingredients are combined thoroughly.
6. Stir in walnuts, granola, and blueberries.
7. Spoon batter into 12 muffin cups.
8. Bake in preheated oven for 15 minutes or until toothpick inserted in center comes out clean.

Nutrition facts
(per serving)

Calories: 184

Total fat: 6 grams

Saturated fat: 1 gram

Sodium: 176 mg

Carbohydrate: 31 grams

Fiber: 3 grams

Protein: 5 grams

Cost: $

*

Blueberry Buckwheat Pancakes

Prep time: 10 minutes / Cook time: 10 minutes / Makes: 16 pancakes / Serving size: 2 pancakes

What you'll need

¾ cup white whole wheat flour
¾ cup buckwheat flour
1½ teaspoons baking powder
½ teaspoon baking soda
¼ teaspoon salt

½ teaspoon ground cinnamon
1 cup low-fat plain yogurt
1 cup fat-free milk
1 tablespoon honey
2 large eggs

2 tablespoons canola oil
2 cups fresh or frozen
  blueberries, divided
½ cup maple syrup

What to do

1. In large bowl, whisk together whole wheat flour, buckwheat flour, baking powder, baking soda, salt, and cinnamon. In medium bowl, beat together yogurt, milk, honey, eggs, and oil. Stir wet ingredients into dry ingredients.

2. Stir in 1 cup blueberries.

3. Preheat large, nonstick skillet over medium heat. Place ¼ cup of mixture into skillet. Flip pancake when it is golden brown on bottom and bubbles are forming on top, about 1 minute. Cook other side until golden.

4. Serve with remaining blueberries and maple syrup.

Nutrition facts
(per serving)

Calories: 243

Total fat: 6 grams

Saturated fat: 1 gram

Sodium: 272 mg

Carbohydrate: 43 grams

Fiber: 3 grams

Protein: 6 grams

Cost: $$

*

Blueberry Oatmeal Scones

Prep time: 10 minutes / Cook time: 20 minutes / Makes: 12 scones / Serving size: 1 scone

What you'll need

¾ cup flour

¾ cup whole wheat flour

1 tablespoon baking powder

1 teaspoon cinnamon, divided

Dash salt

1 cup plus 2 tablespoons rolled oats

2 tablespoons spoonable sugar substitute

3 tablespoons sugar, divided

⅓ cup cold cubed light butter

1 cup fresh or dried blueberries (nutritional analysis based on dried blueberries)

1 beaten egg

½ cup skim milk, plus 2 tablespoons

What to do

1. Preheat oven to 375 degrees.

2. In large mixing bowl, sift flours, baking powder, ½ of cinnamon, and salt. Stir in oats, sugar substitute, and 2 tablespoons sugar. Blend well.

3. Cut in butter and stir until mixture resembles coarse crumbs.

4. Stir in blueberries.

5. Stir in egg and milk.

6. Blend well.

7. Shape dough to form ball and knead dough out on lightly floured work surface.

8. Knead dough about 4 or 5 times.

9. Coat cookie sheet with cooking spray. Place dough onto cookie sheet and pat into circle.

10. Cut dough into 12 slices, similar to cutting a pizza, but do not cut all the way down.

11. Brush scones with remaining milk.

12. In small bowl, stir remaining cinnamon and sugar; sprinkle this mixture over scones.

13. Bake about 20 minutes or until scones have reached a golden brown color.

14. Break scones and serve warm.

Nutrition facts (per serving)

Calories: 163 / Total fat: 6 grams / Saturated fat: 3 grams / Sodium: 115 mg
Carbohydrate: 24 grams / Fiber: 2 grams / Protein: 4 grams / Cost: $$

Blueberry Bread

Prep time: 10 minutes / Cook time: 35 minutes / Makes: 12 slices / Serving size: 1 slice

What you'll need

⅓ cup nonfat vanilla yogurt, plus 1 tablespoon

2 cups mashed banana

3 large eggs

¼ cup canola oil

1½ cups whole wheat flour

1 cup flour

½ cup spoonable sugar substitute

¼ cup dark brown sugar

1 tablespoon baking powder

Dash salt

½ teaspoon cinnamon

2 cups fresh blueberries

¼ cup finely walnuts, chopped

What to do

1. Preheat oven to 350 degrees.

2. Coat large loaf pan with cooking spray; set aside.

3. Blend yogurt, banana, eggs, and oil in large bowl. Add all dry ingredients. Stir in blueberries and walnuts.

4. Stir until blended. Spread batter into prepared loaf pan. Bake for 35 minutes or until cake springs back when lightly touched.

5. Let cool.

Nutrition facts
(per serving)

Calories: 258

Total fat: 8 grams

Saturated fat: 1 gram

Sodium: 122 grams

Carbohydrate: 44 grams

Fiber: 4 grams

Protein: 6 grams

Cost: $

*

Breakfast Casserole with Chicken Sausage

Prep time: 30 minutes / Chill time: overnight / Cook time: 45 minutes / Makes: 6 servings / Serving size: ⅙ casserole

*This dish should be made the night before you want to serve it!

What you'll need

2 teaspoons canola oil

2 cups leeks, rinsed thoroughly, cut in rings

2 links from (12 ounce) package chicken sausage, cut into pieces

¼ teaspoon black pepper

⅛ teaspoon red pepper flakes

¼ teaspoon cayenne

3 large eggs

3 egg whites

1 cup milk (lowfat, 1%, or skim)

½ loaf whole wheat baguette, cut into cubes

½ cup grated sharp 2% cheddar, reduced

1 cup pepper jack cheese, reduced-fat (preferable)

What to do

1. Add canola oil to large, nonstick skillet and turn to medium-high heat. Sauté leeks and chicken sausage with pinch of pepper, red pepper flakes, and ⅛ teaspoon cayenne.

2. When leeks are translucent and sausage is slightly browned, remove from heat and let cool.

3. In separate bowl whisk eggs together with milk, remaining cayenne, and pinch of black pepper.

4. Cut bread into cubes and put in bottom of 9x9-inch glass casserole dish (that has been sprayed with cooking spray). Sprinkle bread with cheddar cheese. Pour sausage and leek mixture and egg mixture on top. Top with pepper jack cheese. Cover tightly and refrigerate overnight.

5. The next morning preheat oven to 375 degrees.

6. Remove casserole from refrigerator and put in middle of oven. Bake for 30 to 45 minutes or until knife is removed cleanly from middle.

7. Remove from oven and allow casserole to stand for 10 minutes before cutting and serving.

Nutrition facts (per serving)

Calories: 236 / Total fat: 11 grams / Sodium: 478 mg / Carbohydrate: 13 grams
Fiber: 2 grams / Protein: 19 grams / Cost: $$ / *

Brown Sugar Pear Muffins

Prep time: 20 minutes / Cook time: 10 minutes / Makes: 36 mini muffins / Serving size: 3 mini muffins

What you'll need

2½ cups whole wheat flour

¾ cup brown sugar, plus a little extra for topping

1 tablespoon baking powder

Dash sea salt

2 teaspoons ground ginger

1 teaspoon cinnamon

½ cup applesauce

1 cup fat-free milk

1 teaspoon apple cider vinegar

⅓ cup canola oil

1 teaspoon vanilla

2 cups pears, chopped

What to do

1. Preheat oven to 375 degrees. Line mini-muffin tins with foil muffin cups.

2. In large bowl, mix flour, sugar, baking powder, salt, and spices. Make well in center and add applesauce, milk, vinegar, canola oil, and vanilla. Stir until mostly combined. Add pears and combine until mixture is well incorporated.

3. Scoop batter into muffin tins. Sprinkle ¼ teaspoon of brown sugar on top of each muffin.

4. Bake for 10 to 12 minutes or until toothpick inserted through center comes out clean.

Nutrition facts
(per serving)

Calories: 152

Total fat: 5 grams

Saturated fat: 0.5 grams

Sodium: 76 mg

Carbohydrate: 26 grams

Fiber: 3 grams

Protein: 3 grams

Cost: $

*

Carrot Couscous Muffins

Prep time: 15 minutes / Cook time: 20 minutes / Makes: 12 muffins / Serving size: 1 muffin

What you'll need

1 cup carrot juice

1 cup dry couscous

1 cup whole wheat flour

1 teaspoon baking soda

1 teaspoon baking powder

1 teaspoon salt

1 teaspoon cinnamon

½ teaspoon nutmeg

1 egg

½ cup brown sugar

¼ cup unsweetened
   applesauce

2 tablespoons skim milk

½ cup Craisins

What to do

1. Preheat oven to 350 degrees. Line 12-cup muffin tin with paper liners.

2. In microwavable bowl, combine carrot juice and couscous. Microwave 4 to 5 minutes until juice is absorbed and couscous is tender. Fluff with fork and set aside to cool.

3. In medium bowl, combine flour, baking soda, baking powder, salt, cinnamon, and nutmeg.

4. In small bowl, whisk together egg, brown sugar, applesauce, and milk.

5. Add egg mixture to dry ingredients and stir until combined.

6. Stir in cooled couscous and raisins.

7. Divide between 12 muffin cups and bake for 15 to 20 minutes or until centers are set and edges are golden.

Nutrition facts (per serving)

Calories: 155 / Total fat: 1 gram / Saturated fat: 0 gram / Sodium: 348 mg
Carbohydrate: 34 grams / Fiber: 2 grams / Protein: 4 grams / Cost: $$ / *

Most loving God, bless this food, the hands that prepared it, and the places from which it came. In Your holy name, amen.

Cornmeal Apple Pancakes

Prep time: 10 minutes / Cook time: 10 minutes / Makes: 18 small pancakes / Serving size: 3 small pancakes

What you'll need

1 cup whole wheat flour

½ cup flour

⅔ cup cornmeal

1 tablespoon baking powder

2 tablespoons sugar

2 tablespoons spoonable sugar substitute

Dash salt

⅓ cup ground flaxseeds

½ teaspoon ground cinnamon

1 egg

2 egg whites

1¾ cup skim milk

1 cup apples, finely diced

¼ cup walnuts, finely chopped

What to do

1. In large bowl, sift flours, cornmeal, baking powder, sugar, spoonable sugar substitute, and salt. Stir in flaxseeds and cinnamon; set aside.

2. Whisk eggs and milk in medium bowl. Pour liquid ingredients over dry ingredients and stir until blended. Add apples and walnuts.

3. Warm large, nonstick skillet to medium heat, spray with cooking spray. Pour batter on skillet to form 4-inch pancake.

4. Cook for about 2 minutes. Flip and cook until golden brown.

5. Repeat with remaining batter.

6. Serve with warm syrup or applesauce if desired.

Nutrition facts (per serving)

Calories: 96 / Total fat: 3 grams / Saturated fat: 0 gram / Sodium: 87 mg
Carbohydrate: 16 grams / Fiber: 2 grams / Protein: 4 grams / Cost: $ / *

Chocolate Chocolate Chip Muffins

Prep time: 20 minutes / Cook time: 20 minutes / Makes: 12 muffins / Serving size: 1 muffin

What you'll need

1¼ cup white whole wheat flour

½ cup unsweetened cocoa powder

1 teaspoon baking powder

½ teaspoon baking soda

¼ teaspoon salt

1 egg

2 egg whites

¼ cup light butter, melted

¼ cup dark brown sugar

¼ cup spoonable sugar substitute

¾ cup skim milk

1 tablespoon canola oil

1 tablespoon pure vanilla

¾ cup mini dark chocolate chips

What to do

1. Preheat oven to 350 degrees.

2. Line 12-cup muffin tin with liners and spray with cooking spray; set aside.

3. Stir flour, cocoa, baking powder, baking soda, and salt in medium mixing bowl. In another mixing bowl, whisk egg and egg whites, then add butter, brown sugar, spoonable sugar substitute, milk, oil, and vanilla.

4. Fold wet ingredients into dry ingredients. Fold in chocolate chips. Be careful to stir mixture just until ingredients are moistened so muffins come out fluffy and not tough.

5. Divide mixture evenly among 12 muffin cups.

6. Bake for 20 minutes or until toothpick inserted in center comes out clean.

7. Serve warm or cold.

Nutrition facts
(per serving)

Calories: 190

Total fat: 9 grams

Saturated fat: 3.2 grams

Sodium: 153 mg

Carbohydrate: 25 grams

Fiber: 2 grams

Protein: 4 grams

Cost: $

*

Fiber Vanilla Bean Milkshakes

Prep time: 5 minutes / Makes: 2 milkshakes / Serving size: 1 milkshake

What you'll need

1½ cups skim milk

1 cup vanilla frozen yogurt

1 tablespoon flaxseeds

½ teaspoon cinnamon

½ cup Fiber One cereal

1 vanilla bean, split lengthwise with seeds removed (discard pod)

What to do

1. Place all ingredients in blender.

2. Blend for about 1 minute or until milkshake is smooth and creamy.

3. Pour into 2 glasses.

Nutrition facts
(per serving)

Calories: 267

Total fat: 8 grams

Saturated fat: 3 grams

Sodium: 221 mg

Carbohydrate: 52 grams

Fiber: 16 grams

Protein: 10 grams

Cost: $

Holiday Breakfast Pies

Prep time: 10 minutes / Cook time: 30 minutes / Makes: 10 breakfast pies / Serving size: 1 breakfast pie

What you'll need

12 ounces ground turkey sausage

¼ cup white onion, minced

1 egg

¼ cup green or red bell pepper, minced

Refrigerated biscuit dough for 10 small biscuits, reduced-fat

3 egg whites

1 ounce skim milk

3 ounces low-fat shredded Colby cheese

What to do

1. Preheat oven to 400 degrees. Coat muffin tin with cooking spray (enough for 10).
2. In large, nonstick skillet over medium-high heat, combine sausage, onion, and bell peppers. Cook until sausage is brown. Drain and set aside.
3. Flatten each biscuit out, then line bottom and sides of 10 muffin cups. Distribute sausage mixture evenly between cups.
4. Mix egg, egg whites, and milk. Pour mixture evenly between cups.
5. Sprinkle with shredded cheese.
6. Bake in preheated oven for about 18 minutes or until filling is set.

Nutrition facts (per serving)

Calories: 144 / Total fat: 5 grams / Saturated fat: 1 gram / Sodium: 562 mg
Carbohydrate: 13 grams / Fiber: 1 gram / Protein: 12 grams / Cost: $ / *

Home-Style Biscuits

Prep time: 5 minutes / Cook time: 12 minutes / Makes: 12 biscuits / Serving size: 1 biscuit

What you'll need

1 cup flour

1 cup whole wheat flour

2 teaspoons baking powder

¼ teaspoon baking soda

¼ teaspoon salt

2 tablespoons sugar

⅔ cup low-fat buttermilk

3 tablespoons plus 1 teaspoon canola oil

What to do

1. Preheat oven to 450 degrees.
2. In medium bowl, combine flours, baking powder, baking soda, salt, and sugar.
3. In small bowl, stir together buttermilk and oil.
4. Pour over flour mixture and stir well.
5. On floured surface, knead dough gently for 12 strokes.
6. Roll dough into ¾-inch thickness.
7. Cut with 2-inch biscuit or cookie cutter, dipping cutter in flour between cuts.
8. Place biscuits on ungreased baking sheet.
9. Bake for 12 minutes or until golden brown.
10. Serve warm.

Nutrition facts
(per serving)

Calories: 92

Total fat: 3 grams

Saturated fat: 0 gram

Sodium: 120 mg

Carbohydrate: 14 grams

Fiber: 1 gram

Protein: 2 grams

Cost: $

*

Lemony Zucchini Bread with Blueberries

Prep time: 10 minutes / Cook time: 45 minutes / Makes: 12 slices / Serving size: 1 slice

What you'll need

1½ cups zucchini, grated

½ cup spoonable sugar substitute

¼ cup sugar

1 egg

1 egg white

¼ cup canola oil

¼ cup applesauce

1½ cups whole wheat flour

½ teaspoon salt

½ teaspoon baking soda

¼ teaspoon baking powder

1 teaspoon ground cinnamon

¼ teaspoon allspice

1 tablespoon fresh lemon zest

2 tablespoons fresh squeezed lemon juice

1 cup fresh blueberries

What to do

1. Preheat oven to 350 degrees.

2. Coat 9-inch loaf pan with cooking spray; set aside.

3. In large bowl, stir together zucchini, sugars, egg, egg white, oil, and applesauce.

4. In separate bowl, sift all dry ingredients (flour, salt, baking soda, baking powder, cinnamon, and allspice).

5. Stir flour mixture into zucchini mixture; stir in lemon zest and lemon juice.

6. Blend well. Fold in blueberries.

7. Pour batter into loaf pan and bake 45 minutes.

8. Let cool 15 minutes before serving.

Nutrition facts (per serving)

Calories: 158 / Total fat: 5 grams / Saturated fat: 0.5 grams / Sodium: 169 mg
Carbohydrate: 27 grams / Fiber: 3 grams / Protein: 3 grams / Cost: $$

Mediterranean Quiche

Prep time: 10 minutes / Cook time: 25 minutes / Makes: 12 mini quiches /
Serving size: 2 mini quiches

What you'll need

1 tablespoon light butter

½ cup onion, chopped

1 zucchini, chopped

4 large mushrooms, sliced

1 clove garlic, minced

2 ounces sun-dried tomatoes packed in oil, drained and chopped

2 tablespoons fresh basil, chopped

1 teaspoon fresh thyme, chopped

Dash salt

⅛ teaspoon ground black pepper

¼ teaspoon crushed red pepper flakes

½ cup egg substitute

¾ cup fat-free half-and-half

2 ounces Gruyère cheese, shredded

3 ounces feta cheese, crumbled

What to do

1. Preheat oven to 375 degrees.

2. In large skillet melt butter over medium-high heat. Add onion, zucchini, mushrooms, and garlic. Cook for about 5 minutes or until vegetables are tender.

3. Add tomatoes, basil, thyme, salt, pepper, and red pepper flakes. Remove from heat and let cool.

4. In bowl, beat egg substitute and half-and-half with wire whisk. Add both cheeses and veggie mixture.

5. Spoon mixture into muffin tin coated with cooking spray.

6. Bake for 20 minutes or until set.

7. Remove from oven and let cool for 10 minutes before serving.

Nutrition facts
(per serving)

Calories: 82

Total fat: 5 grams

Saturated fat: 3 grams

Sodium: 243 mg

Carbohydrate: 6 grams

Fiber: 1 gram

Protein: 6 grams

Cost: $

Morning Turkey Sausage

Prep time: 10 minutes / Cook time: 10 minutes / Makes: 4 patties / Serving size: 1 patty

What you'll need

1 egg white, beaten

¼ cup celery, finely diced

2 tablespoons fresh parsley, chopped

½ teaspoon sage

Dash red pepper

½ teaspoon ground fennel seed

¼ cup onions, finely diced

3 tablespoons quick cooking oats

¼ teaspoon salt

¼ teaspoon black pepper

¼ teaspoon garlic powder

¼ teaspoon onion powder

8 ounces lean ground turkey breast

What to do

1. Coat an unheated large skillet with cooking spray; set aside.

2. Combine all ingredients in large bowl; mix well.

3. Shape into 4 patties.

4. Warm skillet to medium heat.

5. Cook for 5 minutes on each side or until no longer pink.

6. Drain on paper towels.

Nutrition facts (per serving)

Calories: 119 / Total fat: 5 grams / Saturated fat: 1 gram / Sodium: 219 mg
Carbohydrate: 6 grams / Fiber: 1 gram / Protein: 12 grams / Cost: $ / *

Muesli (Granola) Parfaits

Prep time: 15 minutes / Makes: 4 servings / Serving size: ¾ cup muesli, ½ cup berries, 2 tablespoons walnuts

What you'll need

½ cup unsalted raw walnuts

1 cup nonfat milk

1 cup nonfat plain yogurt

1 cup old-fashioned rolled oats

2 tablespoons honey

¼ teaspoon vanilla

2 cups mixed berries, fresh or frozen

What to do

1. Toast walnuts in dry skillet over medium-high heat for about 3 minutes; stir frequently, until fragrant. Chop coarsely.

2. In medium bowl, stir together milk, yogurt, oats, honey, and vanilla.

3. Divide yogurt mixture among 4 cups or parfait glasses.

4. Top each with ½ cup of berries and 2 tablespoons of chopped walnuts.

5. Serve immediately or cover tightly and refrigerate overnight. The parfaits will keep up to 3 days in the refrigerator.

Nutrition facts (per serving)

Calories: 305 / Total fat: 12 grams / Saturated fat: 2 grams / Sodium: 71 mg
Carbohydrate: 41 grams / Fiber: 6 grams / Protein: 11 grams / Cost: $$

Gracious Lord, I thank You for the food that I am about to receive,

for the nourishing You provide, and for the strength You've

given my body. In Your holy name, amen.

Morning Glory Muffins

Prep time: 15 minutes / Cook time: 20 minutes / Makes: 18 muffins / Serving size: 1 muffin

What you'll need

1 cup flour

1 cup whole wheat flour

¾ cup spoonable sugar substitute

½ cup white sugar

1 tablespoon ground cinnamon

¼ teaspoon ground nutmeg

1 teaspoon baking powder

½ teaspoon baking soda

½ teaspoon salt

2 cups carrots, finely grated

1 tart apple, peeled and chopped fine

¼ cup walnuts, finely chopped

1 cup golden raisins

3 eggs

¾ cup apple butter

½ cup canola oil

1 tablespoon vanilla

What to do

1. Preheat oven to 375 degrees.

2. Coat 18 muffin tins with cooking spray; set aside.

3. In large bowl, sift flours, sugars, cinnamon, nutmeg, baking powder, baking soda, and salt. Stir in carrots, apple, walnuts, and raisins.

4. In medium bowl, combine eggs, apple butter, oil, and vanilla.

5. Add this mixture to flour mixture; stir until ingredients are moistened.

6. Spoon batter evenly into prepared muffin cups.

7. Bake at 375 degrees for 15 minutes or until muffins spring back when you touch them in center.

Nutrition facts
(per serving)

Calories: 211

Total fat: 8 grams

Saturated fat: 1 gram

Sodium: 140 mg

Carbohydrate: 33 grams

Fiber: 2 grams

Protein: 3 grams

Cost: $

*

Mushroom and Turkey Bacon Omelet

Prep time: 15 minutes / Cook time: 18 minutes / Makes: 1 omelet / Serving size: 1 omelet

What you'll need

¼ cup onion, chopped

¼ cup green pepper, chopped

3 cloves garlic, minced

1 cup mushrooms, sliced

1 tablespoon light butter

½ cup egg substitute

½ cup shredded reduced-fat cheddar cheese, divided

2 slices turkey bacon, cooked and crumbled

⅛ teaspoon pepper

What to do

1. In large, nonstick skillet, sauté onion, pepper, garlic, and mushrooms in butter. Cook and stir for 5 to 8 minutes or until vegetables are tender and liquid is nearly evaporated.

2. Set aside and keep warm. Pour into skillet coated with nonstick cooking spray. Cook over medium heat for 5 minutes or until bottom is lightly browned. Spoon vegetable mixture over one side; sprinkle with half of cheese and turkey bacon.

3. To fold, score middle of omelet with sharp knife; fold omelet over filling. Transfer to warm platter. Sprinkle with remaining cheese and pepper. Cut in half to serve.

Nutrition facts
(per serving)

Calories: 334

Total fat: 15 grams

Saturated fat: 6 grams

Sodium: 957 mg

Carbohydrate: 13 grams

Fiber: 2 grams

Protein: 37 grams

Cost: $

Oatmeal Pear Delight

Prep time: 25 minutes / Total time: 60 minutes / Makes: 8 servings / Serving size: ½ cup

What you'll need

2 cups rolled oats

⅓ cup walnuts, chopped and toasted

¼ cup hulled pumpkin seeds, toasted

1 teaspoon baking powder

1 teaspoon cinnamon

¼ teaspoon ground ginger

¼ teaspoon cloves

Pinch sea salt

1 egg

2 cups nonfat milk

¼ cup pure maple syrup

1 teaspoon pure vanilla

2 ripe pears, diced

1 tablespoon brown sugar

What to do

1. Preheat oven to 375 degrees. Grease bottom of 10x8-inch baking dish with cooking spray; set aside.

2. Place rolled oats, nuts, pumpkin seeds, baking powder, spices, and salt in medium mixing bowl.

3. In separate bowl, beat egg. Add milk, syrup, and vanilla; stir well to combine.

4. Spread diced pears in an even layer in bottom of baking dish.

5. Pour oat mixture over pears, then slowly pour wet ingredients over oats. Coat top with cooking spray and sprinkle with brown sugar.

6. Bake for 30 to 35 minutes or until oats are lightly browned.

Nutrition facts (per serving)

Calories: 210 / Total fat: 7 grams / Saturated fat: 1 gram / Sodium: 126 mg
Carbohydrate: 30 grams / Fiber: 4 grams / Protein: 8 grams / Cost: $

Oatmeal Raisin Biscuits

Prep time: 10 minutes / Cook time: 13 minutes / Makes: 12 servings / Serving size: 1 biscuit

What you'll need

1 cup whole wheat flour

¾ cup flour

½ cup quick cooking oats

2 tablespoons sugar

½ teaspoon salt

½ teaspoon ground cinnamon

1 teaspoon baking powder

½ teaspoon baking soda

¼ cup light butter, cubed

½ cup raisins

¾ cup low-fat buttermilk

What to do

1. Preheat oven to 400 degrees.

2. In mixing bowl, combine flours, oats, sugar, salt, cinnamon, baking powder, and baking soda.

3. Cut in butter with fork or pastry cutter until mixture resembles coarse crumbs. Stir in raisins and buttermilk until moistened.

4. Knead on floured surface several times.

5. Roll dough on surface to 1 inch thick, use biscuit cutter to make 12 biscuits.

6. Place 1 inch apart on greased cookie sheet or pizza stone and bake for 13 minutes or until biscuits are golden brown on top.

Nutrition facts (per serving)

Calories: 124 / Total fat: 2 grams / Saturated fat: 1 gram / Sodium: 208 mg
Carbohydrate: 24 grams / Fiber: 2 grams / Protein: 3 grams / Cost: $ / *

Peaches 'n' Cream Oatmeal

Prep time: 5 minutes / Cook time: 10 minutes / Makes: 4 servings / Serving size: ½ cup cooked oatmeal, ¼ cup milk, and ¼ of peach mixture

What you'll need

1 cup of rolled oats

1 cup water

1 teaspoon vanilla

½ tablespoon light butter

1 cup fresh or frozen peaches, sliced

¼ cup brown sugar

1 teaspoon cinnamon

1 cup nonfat milk

What to do

1. Cook rolled oats with water according to oatmeal package instructions. Add 1 teaspoon of vanilla when adding oats.

2. Place light butter in medium nonstick skillet. Add peaches and cook until softened, about five minutes. Do not overcook or peaches will lose their shape.

3. Add sugar and cinnamon and cook for 1 minute until syrup forms.

4. Separate oatmeal into 4 bowls and top with equal mixture of peaches.

5. Top each bowl with ¼ cup milk.

Nutrition facts
(per serving)

Calories: 189

Total fat: 4 grams

Saturated fat: 2 grams

Sodium: 39 mg

Carbohydrate: 35 grams

Fiber: 3 grams

Protein: 5 grams

Cost: $

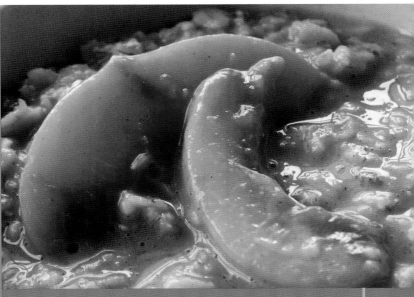

Peanut Butter Cookie Smoothie

Prep time: 5 minutes / Makes: 1 smoothie / Serving size: 1 smoothie

What you'll need

1 cup skim milk

1 medium banana

1 tablespoon cocoa powder

1 tablespoon peanut butter

⅓ cup oats

1½ cups ice

What to do

1. Combine all ingredients in blender.

2. Blend on high speed until drink is very smooth. If you prefer the smoothie sweeter, you can add a touch of honey.

Nutrition facts
(per serving)

Calories: 397

Total fat: 11 grams

Saturated fat: 3 grams

Sodium: 183 mg

Carbohydrate: 65 grams

Fiber: 8 grams

Protein: 18 grams

Cost: $

Pineapple Upside-Down Muffins

Prep time: 15 minutes / Cook time: 20 minutes / Makes: 12 muffins / Serving size: 1 muffin

What you'll need

Topping:
¼ cup dark brown sugar
¼ cup walnuts, chopped fine
1 cup no-sugar-added canned
    pineapple slices, drained
    and cut into 1-inch slices

Batter:
1½ cups white whole wheat
    flour
2 teaspoons baking powder
½ teaspoon baking soda
¼ teaspoon salt
1 tablespoon ground
    cinnamon
¼ teaspoon nutmeg
2 large eggs

½ cup dark brown sugar
¼ cup canola oil
2 tablespoons pineapple juice
1 teaspoon pure vanilla
1 (8 ounce) can undrained
    crushed pineapple
1 cup carrots, grated
½ cup oats
½ cup walnuts, chopped

What to do

1. Preheat oven to 400 degrees. Coat 12-muffin tin with cooking spray.

2. For topping: Sprinkle 1 teaspoon brown sugar into each muffin cup. Sprinkle nuts evenly over sugar. Place pineapple evenly in each muffin cup; set aside.

3. For muffins: Whisk flour, baking powder, baking soda, salt, cinnamon, and nutmeg in large bowl.

4. Whisk eggs and brown sugar in medium bowl until smooth. Whisk in oil, pineapple juice, and vanilla. Stir in crushed pineapple. Add to dry ingredients, stir lightly.

5. Stir in carrots, oats, and nuts.

6. Place batter evenly over 12 muffin cups.

7. Bake for about 20 minutes. Let cool.

8. Flip over muffins and serve upside down!

Nutrition facts (per serving)

Calories: 254 / Total fat: 9 grams / Saturated fat: 1 gram / Sodium: 157 mg
Carbohydrate: 37 grams / Fiber: 3 grams / Protein: 5 grams / Cost: $$

Pumpkin Pie Granola

Prep time: 5 minutes / Cook time: 20 minutes / Makes: 10 servings / Serving size: about ½ cup

What you'll need

3 cups rolled oats

1 tablespoon flaxseed

1 teaspoon cinnamon

½ teaspoon cloves

½ teaspoon nutmeg

5 tablespoons sunflower
   seeds, unsalted

½ cup honey

1 cup canned pumpkin,
   unsweetened

½ cup raisins

⅓ cup dried cranberries

What to do

1. Preheat oven to 350 degrees. Line large cookie sheet with aluminum foil.

2. In large bowl mix oats, flaxseed, and spices.

3. Add in seeds, honey, and pumpkin. Mix until combined.

4. Spread thin layer of mixture on lined cookie sheet.

5. Place in oven for 20 minutes, stirring every 5 minutes or until golden brown.

6. Stir in raisins and cranberries.

7. Serve over milk or yogurt.

Nutrition facts (per serving)

Calories: 239 / Total fat: 4 grams / Saturated fat: 1 gram / Sodium: 6 mg
Carbohydrate: 49 grams / Fiber: 5 grams / Protein: 5 grams / Cost: $

Lord, thank You for this day and the meal I am about to receive.

Let it be nourishment to my body. In Jesus' name, amen.

Pumpkin Bread

Prep time: 10 minutes / Cook time: 35 minutes / Makes: 12 slices / Serving slice: 1 slice

What you'll need

⅓ cup nonfat vanilla yogurt, plus 1 tablespoon

2 cups canned pumpkin

3 large eggs

¼ cup canola oil

1½ cups whole wheat flour

1 cup flour

½ cup spoonable sugar substitute

¼ cup dark brown sugar

1 tablespoon baking powder

1 tablespoon pumpkin spice

Dash salt

¼ teaspoon cinnamon

½ cup golden raisins, chopped

¼ cup walnuts, finely chopped

What to do

1. Preheat oven to 350 degrees.

2. Coat large loaf pan with cooking spray; set aside.

3. Blend yogurt, pumpkin, eggs, and oil in large bowl. Add all dry ingredients. Stir in raisins and walnuts until blended.

4. Spread batter into prepared pan. Bake for 35 minutes or until cake springs back when lightly touched.

5. Let cool.

Nutrition facts
(per serving)

Calories: 120

Total fat: 8 grams

Saturated fat: 1 gram

Sodium: 223 mg

Carbohydrate: 44 grams

Fiber: 4 grams

Protein: 6 grams

Cost: $

*

Pumpkin Spice Muffins

Prep time: 10 minutes / Cook time: 20 minutes / Makes: 12 muffins / Serving size: 1 muffin

What you'll need

Canola oil

1½ cups whole wheat pastry
  flour

½ cup flour

½ cup packed brown sugar

1½ teaspoons baking powder

¼ teaspoon baking soda

¼ teaspoon salt

2 teaspoons cinnamon

1 teaspoon ginger

1 teaspoon nutmeg

½ teaspoon ground cloves

⅓ cup unsweetened
  applesauce

1 cup canned pumpkin

⅓ cup olive oil

⅓ cup nonfat buttermilk

2 large eggs

1 teaspoon vanilla

What to do

1. Preheat oven to 400 degrees. Coat 12-cup muffin pan with canola oil. In large bowl, combine all dry ingredients. Stir well.

2. In medium bowl, combine applesauce, pumpkin, oil, buttermilk, eggs, and vanilla; mix well. Pour liquid mixture into dry ingredients and stir until flour is just moistened—do not beat.

3. Immediately divide batter among 12 muffin cups. Bake for about 20 minutes or until muffins bounce back when pressed lightly.

Nutrition facts
(per serving)

Calories: 196

Total fat: 7 grams

Saturated fat: 1 gram

Sodium: 190 mg

Carbohydrate: 30 grams

Fiber: 1 gram

Protein: 3.5 grams

Cost: $

*

Pumpkin Scones

Prep time: 10 minutes / Cook time: 20 minutes / Makes: 12 scones / Serving size: 1 scone

What you'll need

Scones:

2 cups white whole wheat
   flour
½ cup sugar
1 tablespoon baking powder
½ teaspoon salt
1 teaspoon ground cinnamon

½ teaspoon nutmeg
¼ teaspoon ginger
6 tablespoons cold light
   butter, cubed
¾ cup canned pumpkin
¼ cup fat-free milk
1 large egg

Glaze:

1 cup powdered sugar
1 teaspoon ground cinnamon
2 tablespoons fat-free milk

What to do

1. Preheat oven to 425 degrees. Line baking sheet with parchment paper; set aside.

2. Combine flour, sugar, baking powder, salt, and spices in bowl. With fork, cut butter in to dry ingredients until mixture is crumbly; set aside.

3. In separate bowl, whisk together pumpkin, milk, and egg. Fold wet ingredients into dry ingredients. Form mixture into ball (adding more flour to form into ball).

4. Pat dough onto lightly floured surface and form into 12-inch circle. Use large knife to slice dough, making 12 wedges.

5. Place on prepared cookie sheet.

6. Bake for 20 minutes.

7. For glaze, combine all 3 ingredients and blend well. When scones are cool, drizzle glaze on top.

Nutrition facts (per serving)

Calories: 184 / Total fat: 3 grams / Saturated fat: 1 gram / Sodium: 198 mg
Carbohydrate: 37 grams / Fiber: 1 gram / Protein: 3 grams / Cost: $

Strawberry and Cream Cheese Muffins with Poppy Seeds

Prep time: 10 minutes / Cook time: 25 minutes / Makes: 12 muffins / Serving size: 1 muffin

What you'll need

- 4 ounces (½ block) light cream cheese, softened
- ¼ cup low-sugar strawberry preserves
- 1 cup fresh strawberries, chopped
- 2¼ cups white whole wheat flour
- ⅓ cup spoonable sugar substitute
- 2 teaspoons baking powder
- ½ teaspoon baking soda
- ½ teaspoon salt
- 2 teaspoons poppy seeds
- 1¼ cup low-fat buttermilk
- ¼ cup canola oil
- 1 egg
- 2 egg whites

What to do

1. Preheat oven to 375 degrees.
2. Combine cream cheese, preserves, and strawberries; mix well and set aside.
3. Sift flour, spoonable sugar substitute, baking powder, baking soda, and salt in large bowl. Stir in poppy seeds.
4. In separate bowl, whisk buttermilk, oil, egg, and egg whites. Add to flour mixture; stir just until all ingredients are moistened.
5. Spoon batter ⅓ way full into 12-muffin tin coated with cooking spray.
6. Top each with about 1 tablespoon of strawberry cream cheese mixture. Top with remaining batter. Take long skewer and swirl cream cheese mixture into muffin batter.
7. Bake at 375 degrees for 25 minutes or until muffins are golden brown on top.

Nutrition facts (per serving)

Calories: 211 / Total fat: 8 grams / Saturated fat: 1.5 grams / Sodium: 294 mg
Carbohydrate: 31 grams / Fiber: 1 gram / Protein: 5 grams / Cost: $

Strawberry Basil Scones

Prep time: 10 minutes / Cook time: 10 minutes / Makes: 12 scones / Serving size: 1 scone

What you'll need

2½ cups plus ½ cup white whole wheat flour, divided

¼ cup plus 1 tablespoon sugar, divided

1 tablespoon baking powder

½ teaspoon baking soda

¼ teaspoon salt

½ cup light stick butter, cubed

2 eggs

½ cup plus 3 tablespoons low-fat buttermilk, divided

1 cup fresh strawberries, chopped

¼ cup fresh basil, chopped

What to do

1. Preheat oven to 350 degrees. In large bowl, sift 2½ cups flour, ¼ cup sugar, baking powder, baking soda, and salt. Using fork, cut in butter until mixture resembles crumbs.

2. In medium mixing bowl, whisk eggs and ½ cup buttermilk. Add egg mixture to flour mixture and stir until all ingredients are moistened.

3. Stir in strawberries and basil.

4. Turn dough onto floured work surface (using remaining ½ cup flour). Knead dough about 5 times. Add additional flour if dough is too sticky.

5. Pat dough out into disk shape and transfer to parchment-lined baking sheet.

6. Cut into 12 wedges about ¾ down. Do not cut all the way down.

7. Brush scones with remaining tablespoons buttermilk and sprinkle with remaining 1 tablespoon sugar.

8. Bake for 15 minutes or until golden brown.

Nutrition facts
(per serving)

Calories: 183
Total fat: 6 grams
Saturated fat: 3.5 grams
Sodium: 193 mg
Carbohydrate: 26 grams
Fiber: 1 gram
Protein: 5 grams
Cost: $

Sunshine Smoothies

Prep time: 1 minute / Makes: 2 servings / Serving size: 1 cup

What you'll need

¾ cup orange juice

1 banana

2 cups frozen strawberries

1 cup fat-free vanilla yogurt

1 teaspoon spoonable sugar substitute

What to do

1. Place all ingredients in blender.
2. Blend until smooth.

Nutrition facts
(per serving)

Calories: 222

Total fat: 1 gram

Saturated fat: 0.5 grams

Sodium: 45 mg

Carbohydrate: 53 grams

Fiber: 3 grams

Protein: 4 grams

Cost: $

Sweet Potato Waffles

Prep time: 15 minutes / Cook time: 3 to 8 minutes / Makes: 6 waffles / Serving size: 1 waffle

What you'll need

½ cup whole wheat flour

½ cup flour

¼ cup cornmeal

1 tablespoon baking powder

Dash salt

½ teaspoon cinnamon

⅛ teaspoon ground ginger

⅛ teaspoon nutmeg, freshly grated

1 cup fat-free skim milk

⅓ cup peeled and diced sweet potato, cooked and mashed

2 tablespoons canola oil

1 tablespoon molasses

2 egg whites

What to do

1. In medium bowl, stir flours, cornmeal, baking powder, salt, cinnamon, ginger, and nutmeg.

2. In large bowl, whisk together milk, sweet potato, oil, and molasses.

3. Add flour mixture and stir until blended.

4. Beat egg whites until stiff peaks form, fold into batter.

5. Place mixture in heated waffle iron. Cook until waffle is golden brown, about 3 to 8 minutes depending on size of your waffle iron.

6. Serve with sugar-free maple syrup if desired.

Nutrition facts (per serving)

Calories: 165 / Total fat: 5 grams / Saturated fat: 0.5 grams / Sodium: 253 mg
Carbohydrate: 25 grams / Fiber: 2 grams / Protein: 6 grams / Cost: $ / *

Turkey Sausage Hash Browns

Prep time: 10 minutes / Cook time: 10 minutes / Makes: 4 servings / Serving size: ¼ mixture

What you'll need

1 green bell pepper, diced

¼ cup green onions, thinly sliced

¼ cup onions, chopped

3 cloves garlic, chopped

3 ounces ground turkey sausage

3 cups refrigerated shredded hash brown potatoes

⅓ cup low-sodium chicken broth

1 teaspoon onion powder

1 teaspoon garlic powder

½ teaspoon rubbed sage

⅛ teaspoon pepper

Dash cayenne pepper

Dash salt

What to do

1. Cook pepper, green onions, onions, garlic, and sausage in nonstick skillet over medium-high heat 5 minutes or until browned, stirring to crumble sausage.

2. Add remaining ingredients; cook 5 minutes.

Nutrition facts (per serving)

Calories: 139 / Total fat: 4 grams / Saturated fat: 1 gram / Sodium: 198 mg
Carbohydrate: 22 grams / Fiber: 2 grams / Protein: 6 grams / Cost: $$

Bless, dear Lord, this food to our use and us to

Your service. In Jesus' name, amen.

Tex–Mex Breakfast Burritos

Prep time: 15 minutes / Cook time: 10 minutes / Makes: 10 burritos / Serving size: 1 burrito

What you'll need

10 eggs, lightly beaten
½ teaspoon black pepper
½ teaspoon onion powder
½ teaspoon garlic powder

10 high-fiber, 80-calorie tortillas
1 cup shredded cheddar cheese, low-fat
½ cup green onions, chopped

12 slices turkey bacon, cooked and crumbled
1 cup canned black beans, rinsed and drained
1 cup black bean and corn salsa

What to do

1. Warm large, nonstick skillet to medium heat. Coat pan with nonstick cooking spray.

2. Place all eggs in skillet and cook until eggs are completely set, stirring occasionally, about 3 minutes. Season eggs with pepper, onion powder, and garlic powder.

3. Spoon ¼ cup egg mixture down center of each tortilla; sprinkle each tortilla with cheese, onions, bacon, black beans, and salsa. Fold tortilla.

Nutrition facts
(per serving)

Calories: 262

Total fat: 10 grams

Saturated fat: 3 grams

Sodium: 347 mg

Carbohydrate: 28 grams

Fiber: 6 grams

Protein: 17 grams

Cost: $$

*

Vegetable Omelet

Prep time: 15 minutes / Cook time: 18 minutes / Makes: 1 omelet / Serving size: ½ omelet

What you'll need

¼ cup onion, chopped

¼ cup green pepper, chopped

1 tablespoon light butter

1 small zucchini, chopped

3 cloves garlic, minced

1 small summer squash, chopped

¾ cup tomato, chopped

¼ teaspoon dried oregano

¼ teaspoon dried basil

⅛ teaspoon pepper

½ cup egg substitute

½ cup shredded reduced-fat cheddar cheese, divided

What to do

1. In large, nonstick skillet, sauté onion and green pepper in butter until tender. Add zucchini, garlic, squash, tomato, oregano, basil, and pepper. Cook and stir for 5 to 8 minutes or until vegetables are tender and liquid is nearly evaporated.

2. Set aside and keep warm. Place egg substitute in mixing bowl. Pour into skillet coated with nonstick cooking spray. Cook over medium heat for 5 minutes or until bottom is lightly browned. Bake at 350 degrees for 9 to 10 minutes or until knife inserted near center comes out clean. Spoon vegetable mixture over one side; sprinkle with half of cheese.

3. To fold, score middle of omelet with sharp knife; fold omelet over filling. Transfer to warm platter. Sprinkle with remaining cheese. Cut in half to serve.

Nutrition facts
(per serving)

Calories: 187

Total fat: 9 grams

Saturated fat: 2 grams

Sodium: 300 mg

Carbohydrate: 12 grams

Fiber: 3 grams

Protein: 18 grams

Cost: $

Wheat Waffles with Citrus Compote

Prep time: 10 minutes / Cook time: 5 minutes / Makes: 12 (4 inch) waffles / Serving size: 2 waffles with ⅓ cup compote

What you'll need

Waffles:

¾ cup flour

¾ cup whole wheat flour

¼ cup brown sugar

¼ cup spoonable sugar substitute

¼ cup toasted wheat germ

1¼ teaspoons baking power

1 teaspoon baking soda

¼ teaspoon salt

¼ teaspoon nutmeg

1⅓ cups buttermilk

⅓ cup water

2 tablespoons canola oil

1 teaspoon grated orange rind

1 large egg, lightly beaten

Compote:

¼ cup sugar-free or reduced-sugar orange marmalade

1 tablespoon fresh orange juice

1 teaspoon fresh lemon juice

1 teaspoon honey

2 cups mandarin orange sections

What to do

1. For compote: Place marmalade, orange juice, lemon juice, and honey in small saucepan over medium-low heat; cook 2 minutes or until marmalade melts. Reduce heat and gently stir in orange sections; set aside.

2. For waffles: Combine flours and next 7 ingredients (through nutmeg) in large bowl, stirring with whisk.

3. Combine buttermilk, water, canola oil, orange rind, and egg in small bowl. Add milk mixture to flour mixture, stirring until moist.

4. Coat waffle iron with cooking spray; preheat. Spoon about ⅓ cup batter per 4-inch waffle onto hot waffle iron spreading batter to edges.

5. Cook for 5 minutes or until steaming stops.

6. Serve with ⅓ cup compote.

Nutrition facts (per serving)

Calories: 215 / Total fat: 4 grams / Saturated fat: 1 gram / Sodium: 298 mg
Carbohydrate: 39 grams / Fiber: 2 grams / Protein: 8.5 grams / Cost: $ / *

Whole Wheat Ginger Bread Loaf

Prep time: 5 minutes / Cook time: 30 minutes / Makes: 8 slices / Serving size: 1 slice

What you'll need

1½ cups whole wheat flour

¼ cup dark brown sugar

¾ teaspoon ginger

1 teaspoon cinnamon

⅛ teaspoon cloves, ground

1 teaspoon baking powder

½ teaspoon baking soda

3 egg whites, beaten

½ cup plus 2 tablespoons low-fat buttermilk

½ cup plus 2 tablespoons applesauce, no sugar added

½ cup molasses

What to do

1. Preheat oven to 350 degrees.

2. Coat an 8x8-inch baking pan with cooking spray; set aside.

3. In large bowl, stir flour, brown sugar, spices, baking powder, and baking soda.

4. In small bowl, combine remaining ingredients. Add buttermilk mixture to flour mixture, stir well.

5. Pour batter into prepared pan.

6. Bake for 30 minutes or until cake springs back when you touch it.

Nutrition facts (per serving)

Calories: 187 / Total fat: 1 gram / Sodium: 51 mg / Carbohydrate: 42 grams
Fiber: 3 grams / Protein: 5 grams / Cost: $ / *

Whole Grain Breakfast-Quinoa*

Prep time: 5 minutes / Cook time: 15 minutes / Makes: 6 servings / Serving size: ¾ cup

What you'll need

1⅓ cups quinoa

2⅔ cups water

1 small apple, cored and cut into chunks

¼ cup raisins

½ cup pecans

½ cup low-fat (1%) milk

1 tablespoon (or to taste) spoonable sugar substitute (for example, Splenda)

1 teaspoon vanilla

½ teaspoon cinnamon

6 teaspoons light butter, optional (for topping)

What to do

1. Rinse quinoa under tap in fine mesh strainer. Put rinsed quinoa in saucepan with water. Bring to boil, then reduce heat to simmer. Cover and cook 5 minutes.

2. Add apple chunks and raisins and continue to cook, covered over low heat, until water is absorbed (about 10 minutes more).

3. In meantime, toast pecans in dry skillet over medium-high heat, stirring frequently until fragrant, about 2 to 3 minutes. Allow to cool, then chop.

4. When quinoa is cooked, stir in milk, sugar substitute, vanilla, and cinnamon, and cook until milk is heated through, about 1 minute.

5. Spoon cereal into bowls and top with pecans and butter. Serve with additional sweetener and milk to taste.

*Quinoa (pronounced keen-wah) is a whole grain, and it is one of the best plant sources of protein. This recipe is an excellent source of copper, fiber, folate, magnesium, manganese, protein, and thiamin.

Nutrition facts
(per serving)

Calories: 341
Total fat: 14 grams
Saturated fat: 3 grams
Sodium: 32 mg
Carbohydrate: 38 grams
Fiber: 5 grams
Protein: 8 grams
Cost: $

Zucchini and Carrot Muffins

Prep time: 15 minutes / Cook time: 13 minutes / Makes: 12 muffins / Serving size: 1 muffin

What you'll need

1½ cups whole wheat flour

¾ cup dark brown sugar

¾ cup spoonable sugar
   substitute

1 teaspoon baking powder

½ teaspoon baking soda

1 teaspoon ground cinnamon

¼ teaspoon ground cloves

⅛ teaspoon salt

1 egg

1 egg white

3 tablespoons canola oil

½ cup shredded carrots

1 cup zucchini, grated

1 tablespoon vanilla

¾ cup drained, canned
   crushed pineapple

¼ cup walnuts, chopped

What to do

1. Preheat oven to 350 degrees.

2. Coat 12-muffin pan with cooking spray; set aside.

3. In large bowl, sift flour, sugars, baking powder, baking soda, cinnamon, cloves, and salt together; set aside.

4. In large mixing bowl, combine egg, egg white, oil, carrots, zucchini, vanilla, and pineapple and mix well.

5. Add flour mixture to zucchini mixture. Fold in walnuts.

6. Pour batter into prepared muffin cups.

7. Bake for 13 minutes or until muffins are golden brown on top.

Nutrition facts
(per serving)

Calories: 220

Total fat: 6 grams

Saturated fat: 0.5 grams

Sodium: 109 mg

Carbohydrate: 41 grams

Fiber: 2.5 grams

Protein: 3.5 grams

Cost: $

*

Lunch Recipes

Asian Chicken Slaw

Prep time: 10 minutes / Chill time: 60 minutes / Makes: 6 servings / Serving size: about 1½ cups

What you'll need

2½ cups shredded cooked chicken breast

1 cup celery, finely chopped

½ cup sugar snap peas

½ cup red bell pepper, chopped

¼ cup onion, finely chopped

1 (10 ounce) package slaw

1 (8 ounce) can water chestnuts

¼ cup apple cider vinegar

¼ cup rice wine vinegar

2 tablespoons sugar

1 tablespoon low-sodium soy sauce

½ teaspoon onion powder

½ teaspoon garlic powder

¼ teaspoon freshly ground black pepper

¼ cup slivered almonds, toasted

1 teaspoon sesame seeds, toasted

What to do

1. To prepare slaw, combine first 7 ingredients in large bowl.

2. To prepare dressing, combine cider vinegar and next 6 ingredients (through black pepper) in small bowl; stir with whisk.

3. Pour dressing over slaw; toss to coat. Cover and chill 1 hour.

4. Sprinkle with almonds and sesame seeds before serving.

Nutrition facts (per serving)

Calories: 213 / Total fat: 5 grams / Sodium: 146 mg / Carbohydrate: 22 grams
Fiber: 2 grams / Protein: 20 grams / Cost: $$

Asparagus Orzo Salad with Edamame and Chickpeas

Prep time: 20 minutes/ Makes: 8 servings / Serving size: about ½ cup

What you'll need

Salad:

3 cups cooked asparagus, cut into 3-inch pieces

1 cup shelled edamame, steamed

1 cup cooked chickpeas

1 large red bell pepper, chopped

½ red onion, sliced thin

2 cups cooked orzo pasta

⅛ teaspoon salt

¼ teaspoon ground black pepper

1 teaspoon onion powder

1 teaspoon garlic powder

Vinaigrette:

¼ cup extra-virgin olive oil

3 tablespoons fresh lemon juice

1 tablespoon lemon zest

1 teaspoon dried dill

What to do

1. In large bowl, combine all salad ingredients.
2. In small bowl, whisk all vinaigrette ingredients.
3. Pour vinaigrette over pasta mixture and stir well.
4. Serve hot or cold.

Nutrition facts
(per serving)

Calories: 195

Total fat: 9 grams

Sodium: 43 mg

Carbohydrate: 22 grams

Fiber: 5 grams

Protein: 8 grams

Cost: $$

*

Baked Salmon Salad with Peanut Dressing

Prep time: 20 minutes / Makes: 4 servings / Serving size: 1 fillet, 1 cup spinach, and 2 tablespoons dressing

What you'll need

Salmon:

4 (4 ounce) salmon fillets

2 teaspoons Dijon mustard

1 teaspoon cumin

1 teaspoon paprika

¼ teaspoon crushed red
   pepper

¼ teaspoon salt

½ teaspoon black pepper

Salad:

4 cups spinach

Peanut Dressing:

¼ cup peanut butter

1 teaspoon Asian chili sauce
   (such as Sriracha)

1 tablespoon low-sodium soy
   sauce

1 tablespoon rice wine vinegar

1 tablespoon water

What to do

1. Preheat oven to 350 degrees. Coat foil-lined cookie sheet with cooking spray.

2. Place fillets on baking sheet and coat both sides with cooking spray.

3. Combine mustard and spices; mix well.

4. Top each fillet with ½ teaspoon Dijon mustard and spice mixture.

5. Bake for 10 to 12 minutes, depending on thickness of fillet. (Fish is done when it flakes easily with fork.)

6. For dressing, combine all dressing ingredients and whisk until smooth.

7. Place 1 cup of greens on four plates. Flake cooked salmon over greens using fork. Toss with 2 tablespoons dressing.

Nutrition facts (per serving)

Calories: 261 / Total fat: 15 grams / Sodium: 463 mg / Carbohydrate: 5 grams
Fiber: 2 grams / Protein: 27 grams / Cost: $$$

Broccoli Quiche

Prep time: 20 minutes / Cook time: 45 minutes / Makes: 6 slices / Serving size: 1 slice

What you'll need

1 (11.5 ounce) can refrigerated corn bread twist dough or 1 sheet phyllo dough

1 teaspoon canola oil

½ cup onion, chopped

4 garlic cloves, minced

1 jalapeño pepper, seeded and chopped

½ cup frozen whole-kernel corn

½ cup red bell pepper, chopped

½ teaspoon dried oregano

¼ teaspoon basil

½ teaspoon ground cumin

⅛ teaspoon black pepper

⅛ teaspoon ground red pepper

1 (10 ounce) package frozen broccoli florets, thawed and chopped

1 cup evaporated fat-free milk

2 cups egg substitute

½ teaspoon salt

¾ cup (3 ounces) reduced-fat sharp cheddar cheese

What to do

1. Preheat oven to 350 degrees.

2. Unroll dough; unfold layers (do not separate into strips). Place layers lengthwise, end to end, into an 11x7-inch baking dish coated with cooking spray.

3. Pinch ends in middle to seal; press dough up sides of dish. Set aside.

4. Warm canola oil in large, nonstick skillet over medium-high heat. Add onion, garlic, and jalapeño; sauté 5 minutes or until soft. Add corn and next 7 ingredients (through broccoli); sauté for 5 minutes or until vegetables are soft.

5. Remove from heat. Combine milk, egg substitute, and salt; stir well with whisk. Sprinkle cheese over dough. Spoon broccoli mixture evenly into pan. Pour milk mixture over broccoli mixture.

6. Place dish on baking sheet. Bake at 350 degrees for 45 minutes; cover and bake for an additional 10 minutes or until set.

7. Serve warm.

Nutrition facts (per serving)

Calories: 182 / Total fat: 5 grams / Sodium: 505 mg / Carbohydrate: 15 grams
Fiber: 2.5 grams / Protein: 19 grams / Cost: $$ / *

Butternut Squash Soup

Prep time: 15 minutes / Cook time: 50 minutes / Makes: 6 servings / Serving size: ⅙ of soup

What you'll need

2 large butternut squash, seeded and halved lengthwise

1 tablespoon extra-virgin olive oil

½ teaspoon salt

1 teaspoon ground white pepper

Onion powder and garlic powder to taste

2 tablespoons honey

3 cups reduced-sodium vegetable broth

1 teaspoon fresh ginger, finely chopped

¼ cup half-and-half

Dash nutmeg

What to do

1. Preheat oven to 400 degrees.

2. Brush butternut squash with olive oil and season with salt, pepper, onion powder, and garlic powder.

3. Place squash (cut side down) on foil-lined cookie sheet coated with cooking spray with ½ cup water added to cookie sheet to prevent squash from burning.

4. Place in oven and let squash roast for about 40 minutes.

5. Scoop flesh from skin and place in medium saucepan. Add honey, vegetable broth, and ginger. Bring to simmer. Take away from heat and blend with blender, food processor, or stick blender. Stir in half-and-half and return to simmer.

6. Season to taste with salt, pepper, onion powder, garlic powder, and nutmeg if desired.

Nutrition facts
(per serving)

Calories: 113
Total fat: 3.5 grams
Sodium: 586 mg
Carbohydrate: 21 grams
Fiber: 3 grams
Protein: 1.5 grams
Cost: $$
*

Carrot-Ginger Soup with Roasted Peanuts

Prep time: 15 minutes / Cook time: 20 minutes / Makes: 10 cups / Serving size: 1 cup

What you'll need

2 tablespoons light butter

1½ pounds carrots, peeled and cut into ¼-inch-thick rounds

1¼ cups onion, chopped

1 medium white skinned potato, chopped

2 tablespoons fresh ginger, minced and peeled

¼ teaspoon red pepper

½ teaspoon cumin

½ teaspoon turmeric

5 cups vegetable broth

6 tablespoons peanuts

What to do

1. Melt 2 tablespoons butter in large pot over medium-high heat.

2. Add carrots, onion, potato, and ginger; sprinkle with salt and add spices. Sauté until vegetables are slightly softened, about 10 minutes.

3. Add broth; bring to boil.

4. Reduce heat and simmer until vegetables are soft, about 20 minutes.

5. Cool slightly, then puree in batches in blender until smooth.

6. Return to pot and add more broth if desired to thin soup.

7. Ladle soup into six bowls and top with 1 tablespoon of peanuts.

Nutrition facts (per serving)

Calories: 74 / Total fat: 2 grams / Sodium: 327 mg / Carbohydrate: 13 grams
Fiber: 3 grams / Protein: 3 grams / Cost: $$ / *

Lord, we thank You for these and all our blessings.

Forgive us our sins, in Christ's name we pray. Amen.

Cauliflower Soup with Carrots and Leeks

Prep time: 20 minutes / Cook time: 55 minutes / Makes: 12 servings / Serving size: 1 cup

What you'll need

2 tablespoons extra-virgin olive oil

3 tablespoons light butter

3 leeks, chopped

1 large head cauliflower, chopped

1 cup carrots, chopped

½ cup yellow or white onions, chopped

3 cloves garlic, minced

8 cups low-sodium vegetable broth

Freshly crushed black pepper to taste

½ cup half-and-half

What to do

1. In large stockpot warmed to medium-high heat, add oil and butter. Sauté leeks, cauliflower, carrots, onion, and garlic for 10 minutes, stirring occasionally.

2. Pour in vegetable broth, increase heat to high, and bring to boil.

3. Reduce heat to medium, cover and simmer for 45 minutes.

4. Remove soup from heat. Blend soup with an immersion blender or place soup in large blender or food processor.

5. Season to taste with black pepper if desired. Stir in half-and-half.

Nutrition facts
(per serving)

Calories: 101

Total fat: 6 grams

Sodium: 408 mg

Carbohydrate: 10 grams

Fiber: 3 grams

Protein: 4.5 grams

Cost: $$$

*

Chicken Chowder

Prep time: 20 minutes / Cook time: 20 minutes / Makes: 12 servings / Serving size: $^{1}/_{12}$ mixture

What you'll need

¼ cup extra-virgin olive oil

1 cup carrots, diced

2 large yellow sweet onions, diced

1 cup celery, diced

5 cloves garlic, minced

3 small jalapeño peppers, seeded and diced

1 red bell pepper, diced

⅛ teaspoon salt

½ teaspoon white pepper

1 tablespoon fresh thyme, chopped

3 quarts low-sodium chicken broth

½ cup fresh cilantro leaves

3 cups shredded cooked chicken breast

1 stick light butter

1 cup flour

Dash hot sauce

1 cup fat-free half-and-half

What to do

1. Warm oil in large stockpot over medium heat. Add carrots, onions, celery, garlic, jalapeños, red bell pepper, salt, pepper, and thyme. Sauté for about 10 minutes, stirring occasionally.

2. Add chicken broth, cilantro, and chicken.

3. Melt butter in large skillet over medium-high heat, add flour, and stir with wire whisk to combine. Cook for about 3 minutes, stirring frequently. Ladle about 1 cup of hot broth into skillet, stirring with wire whisk.

4. Add another 2 cups of liquid, stirring to combine. Then add this mixture back to stockpot and cook for about 5 minutes.

5. Remove from heat and stir in hot sauce and half-and-half.

Nutrition facts (per serving)

Calories: 219 / Total fat: 9 grams / Sodium: 166 mg / Carbohydrate: 18 grams
Fiber: 2 grams / Protein: 18 grams / Cost: $$$ / *

Chicken Lettuce Wraps with Almonds and Cranberries

Prep time: 10 minutes / Cook time: 10 minutes / Makes: 6 servings / Serving size: 2 filled wraps

What you'll need

2 tablespoons canola oil, divided

1 pound boneless, skinless chicken breast, cut into ½-inch pieces

1 tablespoon fresh ginger, minced

1 teaspoon garlic, minced

½ teaspoon onion powder

½ teaspoon garlic powder

¼ teaspoon salt

¼ teaspoon ground black pepper

2 tablespoons rice wine vinegar

2 tablespoons reduced-sodium teriyaki sauce

1 tablespoon honey

1 cup dried cranberries

2 cups shredded carrots

½ cup green onions, chopped

⅓ cup toasted almonds, sliced

12 large lettuce leaves

What to do

1. Warm 1 tablespoon oil in large skillet over medium-high heat. Add chicken, ginger, garlic, and seasonings and sauté for about 8 minutes or until chicken is no longer pink in center.

2. In large bowl, whisk remaining canola oil, vinegar, teriyaki sauce, and honey; add this to cooked chicken mixture.

3. Toss in cranberries, carrots, green onions, and almonds.

4. Divide this mixture evenly between 12 lettuce leaves; roll and serve.

Nutrition facts (per serving)

Calories: 217 / Total fat: 8 grams / Saturated fat: 1 gram / Sodium: 263 mg
Carbohydrate: 18 grams / Fiber: 4 grams / Protein: 21 grams / Cost: $$

Chickpea Fritters with Couscous, Grapes, and Walnuts

Prep time: 15 minutes / Cook time: 6 minutes / Makes: 4 servings / Serving size: 2 fritters, ¼ couscous mixture, and 1 tablespoon Greek yogurt

What you'll need

1 cup couscous

⅛ teaspoon salt

¼ teaspoon ground dried cumin

1 cup water

¼ cup walnuts, chopped

1 cup red grapes, halved

½ cup fresh mint leaves, chopped

¼ cup red onion, chopped

1 tablespoon extra-virgin olive oil

1 (16 ounce) can chickpeas, rinsed and drained

¼ cup fresh chives

2 tablespoons green onions, chopped

1 cup fresh flat leaf parsley

½ teaspoon onion powder

½ teaspoon garlic powder

½ cup low-fat Greek yogurt

What to do

1. Combine couscous, salt, and cumin in large bowl. Bring 1 cup of water to boil. Pour boiling water over couscous and cover with plastic wrap. Let stand for 5 minutes.

2. Fluff couscous with fork and add walnuts, grapes, mint, red onion, and olive oil. Cover and set aside.

3. Combine chickpeas, chives, green onions, parsley, onion powder, and garlic powder in food processor. Process until smooth.

4. Form chickpea mixture into 8 patties. Coat large skillet with canola or olive oil cooking spray and heat to medium-high heat.

5. Place fritters on hot skillet and cook for about 3 minutes on each side.

6. Place couscous mixture evenly on 4 plates. Place 2 fritters on top of couscous.

7. Top fritter with 1 tablespoon Greek yogurt.

8. Garnish each plate with fresh mint and parsley.

Nutrition facts (per serving)

Calories: 327 / Total fat: 11 grams / Sodium: 197 mg / Carbohydrate: 47 grams
Fiber: 11 grams / Protein: 14 grams / Cost: $$

Chinese Chicken Salad

Prep time: 20 minutes / Cook time: 8 minutes / Makes: 4 servings / Serving size: ¼ salad mixture

What you'll need

2 tablespoons Hoisin sauce

2 tablespoons reduced-fat peanut butter

2 teaspoons brown sugar

1 teaspoon hot chili paste

1 teaspoon fresh ginger, grated

3 tablespoons rice wine vinegar

1 tablespoon low-sodium soy sauce

1 tablespoon sesame oil

8 wonton wrappers, shredded

½ pound boneless, skinless

chicken breast, cooked and sliced thin

4 cups torn romaine lettuce

2 cups shredded carrots

1 bunch green onions, chopped

¼ cup fresh cilantro, chopped

What to do

1. To prepare dressing, whisk together Hoisin sauce, peanut butter, brown sugar, chili paste, ginger, rice vinegar, soy sauce, and sesame oil.

2. Preheat oven to 375 degrees.

3. Layer shredded wonton wrappers on cookie sheet coated with cooking spray and bake for 8 minutes or until wonton wrappers are golden brown. Cool.

4. In large bowl, combine cooked chicken, wonton wrappers, lettuce, carrots, green onions, and cilantro. Pour dressing over top; toss and serve.

Nutrition facts
(per serving)

Calories: 275

Total fat: 9 grams

Sodium: 479 mg

Carbohydrate: 27 grams

Fiber: 4 grams

Protein: 23 grams

Cost: $$

Coconut Chicken Fingers

Prep time: 5 minutes / Cook time: 12 minutes / Makes: 6 servings / Serving size: about 2 chicken tenders

What you'll need

Chicken:

¾ cup unsweetened flaked coconut, chopped

2 tablespoons flour

⅛ teaspoon ground black pepper

¼ teaspoon garlic powder

2 teaspoons reduced-sodium Creole seasoning

1 pound chicken tenders

½ cup cornstarch

4 ounces egg substitute

Sauce:

½ cup sugar-free apricot preserves

1 tablespoon whole grain mustard

What to do

1. Preheat oven to 350 degrees. Coat large cookie sheet with cooking spray; set aside.

2. In medium mixing bowl, blend coconut, flour, pepper, garlic powder, and Creole seasoning. In separate bowl, toss chicken tenders in cornstarch and shake off. Dip chicken in egg substitute, then roll in coconut mixture. Place chicken onto prepared cookie sheet; repeat process with remaining chicken tenders.

3. Bake in preheated oven for about 12 minutes or until chicken is no longer pink.

4. For sauce, blend both ingredients together.

5. Serve tenders warm with apricot dipping sauce.

Nutrition facts (per serving)

Calories: 331 / Total fat: 22 grams / Sodium: 478 mg / Carbohydrate: 36 grams
Fiber: 3 grams / Protein: 15 grams / Cost: $$

Coconut Shrimp with Pineapple-Mango Salsa

Prep time: 10 minutes / Cook time: 20 minutes / Makes: 4 servings / Serving size: about 7 shrimp with ¼ cup salsa

What you'll need

Coconut Shrimp:

1 pound large shrimp, peeled and deveined

½ cup cornstarch

½ teaspoon salt

½ teaspoon ground black pepper

¼ teaspoon ground red pepper

1 teaspoon garlic powder

½ cup egg substitute

1 ounce unsweetened coconut (about ¾ cup)

Salsa:

1 cup fresh pineapple, finely chopped

1 mango, finely chopped

⅓ cup red onion, finely chopped

¼ cup cilantro, chopped

1 jalapeño, finely chopped

1 lime, juiced and zested

⅛ teaspoon salt

¼ teaspoon pepper

What to do

1. Preheat oven to 400 degrees. Rinse shrimp in cold water, drain and place on paper towels, pat dry.
2. Combine cornstarch, salt, pepper, red pepper, and garlic powder in bowl.
3. Place egg substitute in medium bowl.
4. Place coconut in separate bowl.
5. Working with one shrimp at a time, dredge in cornstarch mixture. Dip in egg substitute, then dredge in coconut.
6. Place shrimp on baking sheet coated with cooking spray.
7. Repeat procedure with remaining shrimp.
8. Lightly coat shrimp with cooking spray.
9. Bake for 20 minutes, turning shrimp over halfway through baking time.
10. For salsa, combine all ingredients in medium mixing bowl.
11. Serve salsa over shrimp.

Nutrition facts (per serving)

Calories: 319 / Total fat: 8 grams / Sodium: 302 mg / Carbohydrate: 35 grams
Fiber: 3 grams / Protein: 28 grams / Cost: $$$

Cranberry Chicken Salad

Prep time: 10 minutes / Chill time: 60 minutes / Makes: 8 servings / Serving size: ⅛ mixture

What you'll need

1 pound chopped cooked rotisserie chicken, skin removed

1 cup celery, chopped

¾ cup red onion, chopped

¾ cup dried cranberries

1 cup reduced-fat poppy seed dressing

⅛ teaspoon salt

½ teaspoon ground black pepper

What to do

1. Combine all ingredients. Chill until ready to serve.

Serving suggestion: Serve with whole grain bread or crackers.

Nutrition facts
(per serving)

Calories: 231

Total fat: 6 grams

Sodium: 496 mg

Carbohydrate: 30 grams

Fiber: 2 grams

Protein: 17 grams

Cost: $$

Eggplant Parmesan

Prep time: 10 minutes / Cook time: 10 minutes / Makes: 8 eggplant slices / Serving size: 1 eggplant slice, 2 tablespoons marinara sauce, and 1 tablespoon Parmesan cheese

What you'll need

1 medium-sized eggplant
1 egg
½ cup skim milk
¼ teaspoon black pepper

1 cup Italian-style breadcrumbs
1 teaspoon oregano
1 teaspoon basil

2 tablespoons olive oil
1 cup marinara sauce
½ cup grated Parmesan cheese

What to do

1. Wash and slice eggplant into 1-inch rounds; set aside.
2. Place egg and milk in small mixing bowl and blend well; set aside.
3. Place breadcrumbs and seasonings in small bowl and set aside.
4. Place large, nonstick skillet over medium-high heat. Add oil.
5. While oil is heating, place each eggplant slice into milk mixture, then dredge in breadcrumb mixture.
6. Place each coated eggplant slice in hot oil. Cook for 3 to 5 minutes on each side, just until golden brown.
7. Place eggplant on serving platter and top with warm marinara sauce and Parmesan cheese.

* Serving suggestion: Serve over hot whole wheat noodles.

Nutrition facts
(per serving)

Calories: 171

Total fat: 8 grams

Sodium: 387 mg

Carbohydrate: 19 grams

Fiber: 4 grams

Protein: 7 grams

Cost: $

*

Fish and Chips

Prep time: 10 minutes / Cook time: 30 minutes / Makes: 4 servings / Serving size: ¼ mixture

What you'll need

2 pounds red potatoes, cut into 8 wedges (choose large red potatoes)

3 tablespoons extra-virgin olive oil

⅛ teaspoon salt

¼ teaspoon freshly cracked black pepper

1 teaspoon onion powder

1 teaspoon garlic powder

⅓ cup light mayo

⅓ cup plain nonfat yogurt

1 tablespoon fresh parsley, chopped fine

2 tablespoons capers, chopped

2 teaspoons whole grain mustard

Dash ground cayenne pepper

¼ cup flour

2 tablespoons cornmeal

⅛ teaspoon salt

⅛ teaspoon pepper

1½ pounds skinless cod fillets, cut into large pieces

2 lemons, cut into 8 wedges

What to do

1. Preheat oven to 450 degrees.

2. On large, nonstick cookie sheet, spread out potatoes. Combine 1 tablespoon olive oil, salt, pepper, onion powder, and garlic powder, and toss until potatoes are evenly coated.

3. Place potatoes in oven for 30 minutes or until golden brown and fork tender. Turn potatoes once halfway through cooking process.

4. In small bowl, combine mayo, yogurt, parsley, capers, mustard, and cayenne pepper to be used as tartar sauce.

5. In medium bowl, combine flour, cornmeal, salt, and pepper. Roll cod in this mixture.

6. In large, nonstick skillet, heat remaining olive oil. Add cod and cook for about 6 minutes or until cod turns white in center, turning over once during cooking process.

7. Serve cod with roasted potatoes, tartar sauce, and fresh lemon wedge.

Nutrition facts (per serving)

Calories: 486 / Total fat: 18 grams / Sodium: 527 mg / Carbohydrate: 45 grams
Fiber: 5 grams / Protein: 37 grams / Cost: $$$

French Leek Pie

Prep time: 15 minutes / Cook time: 30 minutes / Makes: 8 slices / Serving size: 1 slice

What you'll need

1 tablespoon extra-virgin olive oil

3 leeks, washed and chopped

1 cup fat-free half-and-half

8 ounces Gruyère cheese, shredded

1 refrigerated piecrust

What to do

1. Preheat oven to 375 degrees.
2. Put olive oil in large saucepan over medium heat. Stir in leeks. Cook for about 10 minutes or until leeks are soft. Season with salt and pepper if desired.
3. Reduce heat to low and stir in half-and-half and cheese.
4. Pour mixture into piecrust.
5. Bake for 30 minutes or until golden brown on top.
6. Cool for about 15 minutes before cutting.

Nutrition facts (per serving)

Calories: 233 / Total fat: 14 grams / Sodium: 418 mg / Carbohydrate: 22 grams
Fiber: 1 gram / Protein: 6 grams / Cost: $$$ / *

Lord, I thank You for this meal that You have provided for me,

and for all that You do for me. Amen.

Garden Paella

Prep time: 15 minutes / Cook time: 30 minutes / Makes: 12 servings / Serving size: 1 cup

What you'll need

2 tablespoons olive oil

1 large onion, chopped

1½ cups uncooked rice

3 cloves garlic, minced

2½ cups low-sodium
vegetable broth

2 cups carrots, sliced thin

1 cup frozen cut green beans,
thawed

1 red bell pepper, chopped

2 zucchini, chopped

½ teaspoon salt

¼ teaspoon ground turmeric

½ teaspoon ground thyme

1 teaspoon onion powder

1 teaspoon garlic powder

⅛ teaspoon ground black
pepper

⅛ teaspoon paprika

1 (14 ounce) can artichoke
hearts packed in water,
drained and chopped

1 cup tomatoes, chopped

1 cup frozen peas, thawed

1 cup frozen corn, thawed

What to do

1. In large, nonstick skillet, sauté onion in oil over medium-high heat for 3 minutes. Add rice and garlic and sauté for 1 more minute.

2. Add next 12 ingredients and bring to boil. Reduce heat, cover and simmer for 25 minutes or until liquid is absorbed and rice is tender.

3. Stir in artichoke hearts, tomatoes, peas, and corn. Stir until thoroughly heated.

Nutrition facts

(per serving)

Calories: 169

Total fat: 4 grams

Sodium: 101 mg

Carbohydrate: 30 grams

Fiber: 4 grams

Protein: 5 grams

Cost: $$

Grilled Chicken Sandwich with Sun-Dried Tomato

Prep time: 10 minutes / Chill time: 4 hours / Cook time: 20 minutes / Makes: 4 sandwiches / Serving size: 1 sandwich

What you'll need

- 4 (3 ounce) boneless skinless chicken breasts, all fat removed
- 1 tablespoon balsamic vinegar
- 2 teaspoons olive oil, separated
- 3 cloves garlic, minced
- 2 teaspoons fresh thyme, minced
- 1 teaspoon onion powder
- 1 teaspoon garlic powder
- ¼ teaspoon freshly ground pepper
- 1 red onion, sliced thin
- 4 ounces sun-dried tomatoes
- 1 teaspoon Worcestershire sauce
- ¼ teaspoon salt (optional)
- 4 hundred-calorie, high fiber thin hamburger buns (whole wheat, if possible)
- 4 lettuce leaves

What to do

1. Place chicken breasts in shallow dish. Combine vinegar, oil, one clove minced garlic, thyme, onion powder, garlic powder, and pepper and drizzle over chicken. Cover and refrigerate 1 to 4 hours.

2. Coat nonstick covered skillet with cooking spray. Combine onion and remaining garlic with 2 tablespoons water. Cover and cook for 5 minutes until onion is wilted. Uncover and stir until onion begins to brown.

3. Reconstitute sun-dried tomatoes in hot water as per package directions. Drain and chop fine. Place in bowl and add Worcestershire sauce, salt (if using), remaining olive oil, and pepper to taste.

4. Grill chicken, about 5 to 6 minutes per side, turning once. Slice rolls as chicken is cooking, coating rolls with cooking spray and toasting over grill coals.

5. Place bottom half of each roll on plate. Top each roll with lettuce leaf, chicken, and ¼ onion and tomato mixture. Cover with roll tops. Serve immediately.

Nutrition facts (per serving)

Calories: 310 / Total fat: 8 grams / Sodium: 473 mg / Carbohydrate: 37 grams
Fiber: 8 grams / Protein: 27 grams / Cost: $$

Grilled Eggplant Quesadillas

Prep time: 15 minutes / Cook time: 10 minutes / Makes: 6 servings / Serving size: 1 quesadilla

What you'll need

2 eggplants

1 cup sliced roasted peppers, reserve oil for grilling eggplant

8 ounces low-fat, low-sodium shredded Jack cheese

1 bunch fresh basil, chopped

3 tomatoes, chopped

6 (8 inch) whole wheat tortillas

What to do

1. Cut eggplant into ½-inch slices.

2. Brush slices with oil from roasted red peppers.

3. Grill eggplant, basting occasionally with more roasted pepper oil until slices are very soft.

4. Layer cheese, basil, eggplant, tomatoes, and peppers inside tortilla.

5. Fold tortilla in half.

6. Bake tortilla (400 degrees) or cook on hot griddle until center is hot and outside is brown and crisp.

Nutrition facts
(per serving)

Calories: 247

Total fat: 6 grams

Sodium: 488 mg

Carbohydrate: 43 grams

Fiber: 10 grams

Protein: 11 grams

Cost: $$$

Grilled Turkey Burgers

Prep time: 15 minutes / Cook time: 12 minutes / Makes: 4 turkey burgers / Serving size: 1 burger

What you'll need

1 pound lean ground turkey

1 bell pepper, chopped fine

1 small yellow onion, chopped fine

3 cloves garlic, minced

1 egg

¼ cup oats

2 teaspoons steak sauce

1 teaspoon spicy brown mustard

1 tablespoon Worcestershire sauce

½ teaspoon dried thyme

¼ teaspoon pepper

⅛ teaspoon salt

1 teaspoon onion powder

1 teaspoon garlic powder

4 whole wheat hamburger buns

What to do

1. In large bowl, combine all ingredients except buns.

2. Shape into 4 patties.

3. Grill until no longer pink.

4. Serve on buns.

Nutrition facts
(per serving)

Calories: 368

Total fat: 12 grams

Sodium: 464 mg

Carbohydrate: 33 grams

Fiber: 4 grams

Protein: 30 grams

Cost: $$

*

Herbed Pasta Salad

Prep time: 20 minutes / Chill time: 2 hours / Makes: 10 servings / Serving size: $^1/_{10}$ mixture

What you'll need

1 pound wheat bowtie pasta

5 cups fresh broccoli florets

1 cucumber, peeled and sliced thin

1 pint grape tomatoes, halved lengthwise

1 cup olives, sliced

1 (15 ounce) can artichoke hearts, drained and quartered

1 (15 ounce) can chickpeas, rinsed and drained

6 ounces reduced-fat feta cheese, crumbled

Juice and zest of one lemon

½ cup light Italian dressing

1 cup fresh basil, chopped

1 cup fresh flat leaf parsley, chopped

⅛ teaspoon salt

¼ teaspoon pepper

What to do

1. Cook and drain pasta as directed on package. Add broccoli 5 minutes before pasta is done. Rinse with cold water and drain again.

2. Mix remaining ingredients in large bowl; toss with pasta and broccoli.

3. Serve warm or cold.

Nutrition facts (per serving)

Calories: 198 / Total fat: 6 grams/ Sodium: 396 mg / Carbohydrate: 30 grams
Fiber: 6.5 grams / Protein: 9 grams / Cost: $$$

Bounteous God, for lush fields, succulent fruits, and hearty grains,

I give You thanks today. Amen.

Lentil, Corn, and Tomato Salad

Prep time: 15 minutes / Cook time: 30 minutes / Makes: 8 servings / Serving size: ⅛ mixture

What you'll need

1 cup dry lentils

1 bay leaf

1 sprig fresh thyme

¼ cup extra-virgin olive oil, divided

1 cup red onion, diced

1 cup carrots, diced

3 cloves garlic, minced

1 cup fresh corn kernels

1 cup cherry tomatoes, quartered

½ cup flat leaf parsley, chopped

¼ cup fresh basil, chopped

⅛ teaspoon salt

¼ teaspoon black pepper

Juice of 1 large lemon

What to do

1. In saucepan, combine lentils, bay leaf, and thyme. Cover lentils with water and bring to boil. Reduce heat to medium low and simmer for about 20 minutes or until lentils are tender.

2. Drain lentils and remove bay leaf and thyme.

3. In large, nonstick skillet heated to medium-high heat, add 2 tablespoons olive oil. Add onion, carrot, and garlic to skillet and sauté vegetables for about 4 minutes. Add corn and sauté an additional 3 minutes. Stir in tomatoes, parsley, and basil and cook for 2 more minutes, stirring occasionally. Season with salt and pepper to taste, if desired. Add corn mixture to drained lentils. Add lemon juice and remaining olive oil, stir well.

4. Serve at room temperature, heated or chilled.

Nutrition facts
(per serving)

Calories: 190

Total fat: 7 grams

Sodium: 59 mg

Carbohydrate: 25 grams

Fiber: 9 grams

Protein: 8 grams

Cost: $$

Marinated Grilled Chicken Breast with Watermelon-Jalapeño Salsa

Prep time: 20 minutes / Chill time: 4 hours / Cook time: 10 minutes / Makes: 4 servings / Serving size: 1 chicken breast half and 1 cup salsa

What you'll need

Chicken:

1 teaspoon dried oregano

1 teaspoon dried basil

1 tablespoon extra-virgin olive oil

1 teaspoon chili powder

1 teaspoon cumin

¼ teaspoon salt

3 garlic cloves, minced

1 teaspoon onion powder

1 teaspoon garlic powder

4 (6 ounce) skinless, boneless chicken breast halves

Salsa:

2 cups cubed (½ inch) seeded watermelon

1 cup cubed (½ inch) peeled ripe mango

1 tablespoon fresh lime juice

¼ cup red onion, finely chopped

2 tablespoons fresh cilantro, chopped

1 tablespoon jalapeño pepper (about 1 small pepper), finely chopped and seeded

1 tablespoon fresh lime zest

½ teaspoon sugar

¼ teaspoon salt

What to do

1. Combine first 9 ingredients in large zip-top bag. Add chicken to bag; seal. Marinate in refrigerator up to 4 hours, turning bag occasionally.

2. Prepare grill.

3. Place chicken on grill rack coated with cooking spray. Grill 5 minutes on each side or until done.

4. Combine watermelon and remaining salsa ingredients. Serve watermelon mixture with chicken.

Nutrition facts (per serving)

Calories: 280 / Total fat: 6 grams / Sodium: 412 mg / Carbohydrate: 16 grams
Fiber: 2 grams / Protein: 40 grams / Cost: $$

Minestrone Soup

Prep time: 20 minutes / Cook time: 35 minutes / Makes: 10 servings / Serving size: 1 cup

What you'll need

2 tablespoons olive oil

1 large onion, chopped

3 medium carrots, chopped

3 stalks celery, chopped

4 cloves garlic, chopped

1 can navy beans, drained and rinsed

1 potato, cubed

2 (15 ounce) cans diced tomatoes

2 zucchini, sliced

1 can green beans, drained and rinsed

¼ teaspoon black pepper

⅛ teaspoon salt

3 cups reduced-sodium vegetable broth

1 tablespoon dried basil

1 cup cooked macaroni noodles, whole wheat

3 cups water

What to do

1. Warm oil in large stockpot over medium-high heat. Add onion, carrots, celery, and garlic. Sauté for 5 minutes. Add navy beans, potato, tomatoes, zucchini, green beans, pepper, salt, broth, basil, pasta, and water. Reduce heat and simmer 30 minutes.

2. Add more water if necessary.

Nutrition facts
(per serving)

Calories: 160

Total fat: 4 grams

Sodium: 388 mg

Carbohydrate: 27 grams

Fiber: 6 grams

Protein: 8 grams

Cost: $$

*

Mediterranean Shrimp and Pasta Salad

Prep time: 10 minutes / Cook time: 10 minutes / Makes: 5 servings / Serving size: 1½ cups

What you'll need

Vinaigrette:
¼ cup extra-virgin olive oil
¼ cup lemon juice
2 tablespoons sherry vinegar
1 teaspoons Dijon mustard
⅛ teaspoon salt
½ teaspoon freshly ground
   black pepper
6 fresh basil leaves, finely
   chopped

Salad:
6 cups water
2 bay leaves
1 pound raw shrimp
4 cups whole wheat rotini
   pasta
⅛ teaspoon salt
¼ teaspoon ground black
   pepper
1 cup arugula

1 zucchini, halved lengthwise
   and sliced thin
1 yellow bell pepper, sliced
   thin
3 ounces reduced-fat feta
   cheese
½ cup red onion, sliced thin
¼ cup flat leaf parsley,
   chopped
¼ cup fresh basil, chopped

What to do

1. For vinaigrette, combine all ingredients except basil in medium mixing bowl. Whisk, then stir in fresh basil leaves and set aside.

2. For salad, combine water and bay leaves in large saucepan; bring to boil. Add shrimp; cook 3 minutes or until pink.

3. Drain shrimp and rinse well. Discard bay leaves. Peel shrimp; cover and chill.

4. Cook pasta according to package directions, omitting salt and fat; drain and rinse pasta under cool water.

5. Combine shrimp, pasta, and remaining ingredients in large bowl.

6. Drizzle vinaigrette over salad.

7. Toss gently to coat.

Nutrition facts (per serving)

Calories: 379 / Total fat: 14 grams / Sodium: 376 mg / Carbohydrate: 37 grams
Fiber: 5 grams / Protein: 27 grams / Cost: $$$

Mexican Taco Salad

Prep time: 20 minutes / Cook time: 10 minutes / Makes: 6 servings / Serving size: ⅙ mixture

What you'll need

1 pound lean ground beef

1 cup onion, chopped

1 cup salsa

¾ cup water

1 tablespoon chili powder

1 teaspoon cumin

½ teaspoon onion powder

½ teaspoon garlic powder

¼ teaspoon salt

Dash cayenne pepper

1 can kidney beans, rinsed and drained

1 can green chilies, diced

3 cups baked tortilla chips

6 cups torn romaine lettuce

¾ cup shredded 2% cheddar cheese

What to do

1. Cook beef and onion until beef is browned; drain. Stir in salsa, water, and all seasonings. Bring to boil. Reduce heat to low and simmer for 4 minutes.

2. Stir in beans and chilies.

3. Layer ingredients on six individual plates: ½ cup tortilla chips, 1 cup lettuce, ¾ cup meat mixture, and 2 tablespoons cheese. Serve with additional salsa or taco sauce if desired.

Nutrition facts (per serving)

Calories: 329 / Total fat: 11 grams / Sodium: 509 mg / Carbohydrate: 32 grams
Fiber: 6 grams / Protein: 27 grams / Cost: $$$

Lord, I thank You for this food I'm about to receive. Allow it to nourish my body, and let my body be of service to You. Amen.

Panzanella Summer Salad

Prep time: 10 minutes / Cook time: 20 minutes / Makes: 4 servings / Serving size: 1 cup romaine lettuce, 1½ cups bean mixture, and 2 tablespoons feta cheese

What you'll need

2 cups whole wheat baguette, cubed

1 tablespoon lemon juice

1 tablespoon olive oil

1 teaspoon oregano

1 (15.5 ounce) can garbanzo beans, rinsed and drained

1 cup cucumber, chopped

2 cups cherry tomatoes, quartered

½ cup red bell pepper, chopped

¼ cup fresh parsley, finely chopped

½ cup fresh basil, finely chopped

4 cups romaine lettuce, chopped

½ cup feta cheese, reduced fat

What to do

1. Preheat oven to 350 degrees. Place cubed baguette on foil-lined cookie sheet. Toast bread until slightly brown on top, about 5 minutes.

2. In medium-sized bowl, whisk together lemon juice, olive oil, and oregano.

3. Add beans, cucumber, tomatoes, and red pepper to bowl and toss.

4. Place mixture in refrigerator and allow to marinate for 1 hour.

5. Add cubed bread, parsley, and basil.

6. Serve bean mixture over 1 cup romaine lettuce and top with feta cheese.

Nutrition facts
(per serving)

Calories: 311

Total fat: 9 grams

Sodium: 361 mg

Carbohydrate: 45 grams

Fiber: 11 grams

Protein: 14 grams

Cost: $

Pasta with Artichokes and Sun-Dried Tomatoes

Prep time: 15 minutes / Cook time: 5 minutes / Makes: 8 servings / Serving size: ⅛ mixture

What you'll need

2 tablespoons olive oil

2 tablespoons crushed garlic

½ cup onions, chopped

2 cups canned artichoke hearts, chopped

½ cup capers

1 cup sun-dried tomatoes packed in oil, drained and chopped

¼ cup lemon juice

½ cup cooking wine

1 teaspoon garlic powder

1 teaspoon onion powder

⅛ teaspoon salt

¼ teaspoon crushed black pepper

4 cups cooked whole wheat penne pasta

½ cup shredded Parmesan cheese

What to do

1. In large skillet, heat olive oil to medium high. Add garlic and onions and sauté for 3 minutes. Add artichokes, tomatoes, and capers. Cook for 1 minute.

2. Pour in lemon juice, cooking wine, and all seasonings.

3. Toss in pasta and heat thoroughly.

4. Sprinkle Parmesan cheese over pasta.

Nutrition facts (per serving)

Calories: 202 / Total fat: 5 grams / Sodium: 484 mg / Carbohydrate: 33 grams
Fiber: 4 grams / Protein: 8 grams / Cost: $$ / *

Pumpkin-Black Bean Soup

Prep time: 15 minutes / Cook time: 30 minutes / Serves: 6 / Serving size: 1 cup soup, 1 tablespoon cheese, 1 tablespoon green onions, 1 teaspoon pumpkin seeds

What you'll need

1 teaspoon olive oil

1½ cup onion, chopped

½ teaspoon cumin

1 garlic clove, minced

2 (15 ounce) cans no-salt-added black beans

1 (10 ounce) can Rotel tomatoes, hot

1 (15 ounce) can no-salt-added, diced tomatoes drained

3 cups fat-free, low-sodium chicken broth

½ teaspoon black pepper

1 (15 ounce) can pumpkin

½ cup feta cheese

½ cup green onions, sliced

Pumpkin seeds for garnish

What to do

1. Warm oil in pan over medium-high heat.
2. Add onion to pan and sauté for 5 minutes or until lightly browned.
3. Add cumin and garlic; sauté for 1 minute.
4. Add beans, tomatoes, broth, pepper, and pumpkin.
5. Bring mixture to boil.
6. Cover, reduce heat, and simmer for 20 minutes.
7. Ladle 1 cup into 6 bowls and garnish with 2 tablespoons cheese, 1 tablespoon green onions, and 1 teaspoon pumpkin seeds.

Nutrition facts
(per serving)

Calories: 230

Total fat: 5 grams

Sodium: 347 mg

Carbohydrate: 36 grams

Fiber: 11 grams

Protein: 14 grams

Cost: $

*

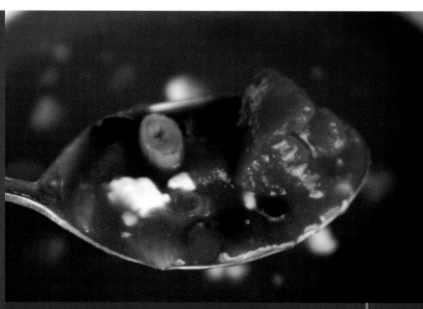

Pumpkin Quesadillas with Cranberry Orange Salsa

Prep time: 10 minutes / Cook time: 25 minutes / Makes: 4 servings / Serving size: 1 quesadilla and 2 tablespoons salsa

What you'll need

Quesadillas:

1 tablespoon vegetable oil

1½ cups peeled and seeded pumpkin or winter squash, cubed

1 medium onion, chopped

1 small red bell pepper, chopped

1 large tomato, chopped

½ cup cooked corn

½ teaspoon ground cumin

½ teaspoon ground coriander

½ teaspoon chili powder

⅛ teaspoon salt

8 small corn tortillas

¾ cup low-fat Monterey Jack

Salsa:

1 navel orange, zest and fruit

¼ cup whole cranberries

2 tablespoons pecans

1 tablespoon spoonable sugar substitute

What to do

1. Preheat oven to 450 degrees.

2. Warm oil in large, nonstick skillet over high heat. Add pumpkin and cook for 2 minutes, stirring often. Add onions and peppers and cook for an additional 2 minutes. Stir in tomato, corn, and spices, cooking for 2 minutes.

3. Transfer vegetables to foil-lined cookie sheet and roast in oven for 8 to 10 minutes or until pumpkin is tender when pierced with fork.

4. Warm large skillet over medium heat and spray with cooking spray. Add 1 tortilla, sprinkling surface with cheese. Top with ¼ cup pumpkin mixture, additional cheese, and another tortilla. Flip tortilla after about 45 seconds and heat other side. Repeat for remaining three quesadillas.

5. For salsa, zest 1 orange directly into food processor. Add cranberries, pecans, and peeled and quartered orange. Blend until chunky (do not puree).

6. Serve salsa over warm quesadillas.

Nutrition facts (per serving)

Calories: 298 / Total fat: 9 grams / Sodium: 209 mg / Carbohydrate: 36 grams
Fiber: 6 grams / Protein: 11 grams / Cost: $$

Quinoa and Black Beans

Prep time: 10 minutes / Cook time: 35 minutes / Makes: 10 servings / Serving size: about ½ cup

What you'll need

1 teaspoon olive oil

1 large onion, chopped

1 large red bell pepper, chopped

3 cloves garlic, chopped fine

¾ cup uncooked quinoa

1½ cups vegetable broth

1 teaspoon ground cumin

1 teaspoon onion powder

1 teaspoon garlic powder

½ teaspoon ground red pepper

⅛ teaspoon sea salt

¼ teaspoon ground black pepper

1 cup frozen or fresh corn kernels

2 (15 ounce) cans black beans, rinsed and drained

¼ cup fresh cilantro, chopped

What to do

1. Warm oil in medium saucepan over medium heat. Add onion, bell pepper, and garlic and sauté for 5 minutes.

2. Mix quinoa and vegetable broth into saucepan. Season with cumin, onion powder, garlic powder, red pepper, salt, and pepper. Bring to boil. Cover, reduce heat, and simmer for 20 minutes.

3. Stir corn into saucepan, add onion and bell pepper mixture, and continue to simmer about 5 minutes until heated through.

4. Stir in black beans and cilantro and simmer until black beans are thoroughly heated.

Nutrition facts
(per serving)

Calories: 149

Total fat: 2 grams

Sodium: 174 mg

Carbohydrate: 27 grams

Fiber: 6 grams

Protein: 7 grams

Cost: $

Sesame Noodle Salad with Red Bell Peppers, Sprouts, and Peanuts

Prep time: 15 minutes / Chill time: 30 minutes / Makes: 4 servings / Serving size: 1¼ cups

What you'll need

Dressing:

¼ cup fresh squeezed lime juice

2 tablespoons low-sodium soy sauce

1 tablespoon dark brown sugar

1 tablespoon water

1 tablespoon sesame oil

1 tablespoon red curry paste

1 tablespoon fresh ginger, grated

1 tablespoon canola oil

⅛ teaspoon salt

¼ teaspoon pepper

Salad:

8 ounces cooked whole wheat spaghetti, drained and rinsed under cold water

2 cups fresh bean spouts

2 cups fresh baby spinach leaves, chopped

1 large red bell pepper, sliced thin

¼ cup green onions, chopped

¼ cup fresh cilantro, chopped

1 ounce peanuts, finely chopped

What to do

1. For dressing, combine all dressing ingredients in large metal bowl. Whisk until blended well; set aside.

2. For salad, combine all salad ingredients except peanuts. Pour dressing over pasta mixture and mix well.

3. Chill in refrigerator for at least 30 minutes.

4. Sprinkle with peanuts.

Nutrition facts (per serving)

Calories: 231 / Total fat: 11 grams / Sodium: 365 mg / Carbohydrate: 29 grams
Fiber: 6 grams / Protein: 8 grams / Cost: $$

Shrimp Cakes with Avocado and Tomato Salsa

Prep time: 20 minutes / Cook time: 8 minutes / Makes: 8 shrimp cakes and 2 cups salsa / Serving size: 1 shrimp cake with ¼ cup salsa

What you'll need

Shrimp cakes:

1 pound raw shrimp, peeled and deveined

1 shallot, diced

½ cup white onion, chopped

½ cup celery, chopped

3 tablespoons cilantro

1 egg white

Juice of 1 lemon

1 teaspoon sesame oil

1 tablespoon low-sodium soy sauce

⅛ teaspoon salt

¼ teaspoon crushed black pepper

1 cup panko breadcrumbs

2 tablespoons olive oil

Salsa:

1 avocado, diced

4 Roma tomatoes, seeded and diced

2 tablespoons cilantro

¼ cup red onion, finely diced

2 cloves garlic, finely chopped

Juice of 1 lime

¼ teaspoon crushed black pepper

⅛ teaspoon salt

What to do

1. In blender or food processor, combine shrimp, shallot, onion, celery, cilantro, egg white, lemon juice, sesame oil, soy sauce, salt, and pepper. Process until mixture is chunky, but do not puree.

2. Place mixture in large bowl. Add breadcrumbs.

3. Form mixture into 8 patties.

4. In large, nonstick skillet heated to medium high, add olive oil. Brown shrimp cakes for 4 minutes on each side or until both sides are golden brown.

5. Combine all salsa ingredients in medium mixing bowl.

6. Serve shrimp cakes topped with salsa.

Nutrition facts (per serving)

Calories: 202 / Total fat: 8 grams / Sodium: 503 mg / Carbohydrate: 17 grams
Fiber: 3 grams / Protein: 15 grams / Cost: $$$

Shrimp Florentine

Prep time: 15 minutes / Cook time: 7 minutes / Makes: 4 servings / Serving size: 1½ cups

What you'll need

1 teaspoon olive oil

1 pound medium shrimp, peeled and deveined

5 cloves garlic, minced

1 teaspoon light butter

¾ cup fat-free half-and-half

⅓ cup low-sodium chicken broth

⅓ cup grated Parmesan cheese

¼ teaspoon crushed red pepper flakes

¼ teaspoon black pepper

1 teaspoon garlic powder

1 teaspoon onion powder

3 cups frozen chopped spinach, drained and squeezed dry

1 (15 ounce) can diced tomatoes, drained

3 cups whole wheat fettuccini noodles, cooked

What to do

1. In medium saucepan on medium heat, add oil. When oil is hot, add shrimp and garlic. Cook for 4 minutes. Remove from pan and keep warm.

2. Melt butter in pan over medium heat. Stir in half-and-half, broth, cheese, and seasonings. Cook 2 minutes, stirring well with wire whisk.

3. Stir in shrimp, spinach, and diced tomatoes; cook 1 minute.

4. Place pasta in large bowl and pour mixture over pasta.

5. Serve immediately.

Nutrition facts (per serving)

Calories: 363 / Total fat: 8 grams / Sodium: 454 mg/ Carbohydrate: 41 grams
Fiber: 9 grams / Protein: 36 grams / Cost: $$

Smoked Gouda Macaroni and Cheese

Prep time: 10 minutes / Cook time: 25 minutes / Makes: 8 servings / Serving size: just under ¾ cup

What you'll need

1 slice whole wheat bread

1 tablespoon light butter

¼ cup green onions, thinly sliced

2 garlic cloves, minced

2 tablespoons flour

2 cups fat-free milk

½ teaspoon salt

¼ teaspoon black pepper

½ teaspoon onion powder

½ teaspoon garlic powder

½ cup (2 ounces) shredded smoked Gouda cheese

⅓ cup (about 1½ ounces) grated reduced-fat Parmesan cheese

5 cups fresh spinach, coarsely chopped

4 cups hot cooked whole wheat elbow macaroni (about 2 cups uncooked)

What to do

1. Preheat oven to 350 degrees. Place bread in food processor and pulse 10 times or until coarse crumbs measure ½ cup. Melt butter in large saucepan over medium heat. Add onions and garlic; cook 1 minute.

2. Add flour; cook 1 minute, stirring constantly. Gradually add milk, salt, pepper, onion powder, and garlic powder, stirring constantly with whisk until blended. Bring to boil; cook until thick (about 2 minutes). Add cheeses; stir until melted. Add spinach and macaroni to cheese sauce, stirring until well blended. Spoon mixture into 2-quart baking dish coated with cooking spray. Sprinkle with breadcrumbs.

3. Bake at 350 degrees for 15 minutes or until bubbly.

Nutrition facts
(per serving)

Calories: 183

Total fat: 5 grams

Sodium: 349 mg

Carbohydrate: 27 grams

Fiber: 3 grams

Protein: 10 grams

Cost: $

*

Southwestern White Chili

Prep time: 10 minutes / Cook time: 20 minutes / Makes: 6 servings / Serving size: 1 cup

What you'll need

2 tablespoons low-sodium Italian dressing

1 pound boneless, skinless chicken breasts cut into bite-sized pieces

3 cloves garlic, chopped

1 small onion, chopped

2 (15 ounce) cans white beans, rinsed and drained

1 (14.5 ounce) can fat-free, reduced-sodium chicken broth

1 (4 ounce) can green chilies, undrained

1 teaspoon ground cumin

1 teaspoon garlic powder

1 teaspoon onion powder

1½ cups reduced-fat pepper jack cheese

2 tablespoons fresh cilantro, chopped

What to do

1. Warm dressing in large saucepan on medium-high heat. Add chicken, garlic, and onion; cook 7 minutes or until chicken is cooked through, stirring occasionally.

2. Stir in beans, broth, chilies, cumin, garlic powder, and onion powder. Bring to boil.

3. Reduce heat to medium low; simmer 10 minutes, stirring occasionally.

4. Serve topped with cheese and cilantro.

Nutrition facts
(per serving)

Calories: 320

Total fat: 8 grams

Sodium: 420 mg

Carbohydrate: 26 grams

Fiber: 6 grams

Protein: 35 grams

Cost: $$

Southwestern Egg Rolls

Prep time: 15 minutes / Cook time: 30 minutes / Makes: 10 egg rolls / Serving size: 1 egg roll

What you'll need

- ¼ cup extra-virgin olive oil, divided
- ¼ cup green onions, chopped
- ¼ cup red bell pepper, chopped
- 3 cloves garlic, chopped
- 4 fresh jalapeño peppers, chopped fine
- 1 cup frozen whole kernel corn
- ½ cup cooked black beans
- 2 tablespoons fresh cilantro, chopped
- ½ cup frozen spinach, thawed and drained
- 1 teaspoon ground cumin
- 1 teaspoon onion powder
- 1 teaspoon garlic powder
- 1 teaspoon chili powder
- ¼ teaspoon cayenne pepper
- ⅛ teaspoon salt
- 12 ounces boneless, skinless chicken breasts, cooked and cut into small chunks
- 1 cup shredded low-fat Monterey Jack cheese
- 10 (8 inch) flour tortillas

What to do

1. Warm 1 tablespoon olive oil in large, nonstick skillet over medium-high heat. Stir in green onion, bell pepper, garlic, and jalapeño peppers. Cook for 3 minutes.

2. Stir in corn, black beans, cilantro, and spinach. Cook an additional 2 minutes.

3. Stir in all seasonings and cook until vegetables have desired tenderness, about 3 minutes. Stir in cooked chicken.

4. Remove from heat and stir in shredded Monterey Jack cheese.

5. Microwave tortillas for about 30 seconds so they are easy to fold.

6. Spoon equal amounts of mixture into each tortilla. Fold ends of tortilla, then roll tightly around mixture. Secure with toothpicks, if needed.

7. Place 1 tablespoon olive oil back in nonstick skillet, heated to medium high.

8. Add stuffed tortillas 3 at a time. Cook for about 3 minutes on each side. Repeat with remaining oil and tortillas.

9. Cut in half and serve immediately.

Nutrition facts (per serving)

Calories: 356 / Total fat: 17 grams / Sodium: 503 mg / Carbohydrate: 38 grams
Fiber: 2 grams / Protein: 14 grams / Cost: $$ / *

Spaghetti with Red Sauce and Fresh Mushrooms

Prep time: 15 minutes / Cook time: 20 minutes / Makes: 6 servings / Serving size: 3 ounces spaghetti with ⅙ sauce mixture

What you'll need

1 tablespoon olive oil

½ cup onions, chopped

2 cloves garlic, minced

2 pounds mushrooms, variety of your choice

1 (16 ounce) can tomatoes, crushed

1 tablespoon tomato paste

1 tablespoon snipped fresh basil

1 tablespoon snipped fresh parsley

1 teaspoon sugar substitute

1 teaspoon dried oregano

½ teaspoon dried thyme

½ teaspoon light salt

½ teaspoon ground black pepper

12 ounces spaghetti, whole wheat

What to do

1. Coat unheated large skillet with olive oil. Over medium-high heat, add onions and garlic and cook for 3 minutes.

2. Coarsely chop 1 pound of mushrooms; slice remaining mushrooms.

3. Add chopped and sliced mushrooms to sautéed onions. Cook and stir for 15 minutes or until mushrooms turn brown.

4. Stir in tomatoes (with juice), tomato paste, basil, parsley, sugar substitute, oregano, thyme, salt, and pepper. Bring to boil. Reduce heat and simmer for 10 minutes.

5. Meanwhile, cook pasta according to package directions. Drain pasta and serve sauce on top of whole wheat pasta noodles.

Nutrition facts (per serving)

Calories: 274 / Total fat: 2 grams / Sodium: 308 mg / Carbohydrate: 56 grams
Fiber: 3 grams / Protein: 15 grams / Cost: $$ / *

Spicy Chicken Quesadillas

Prep time: 15 minutes / Cook time: 15 minutes / Makes: 8 servings / Serving size: 1 quesadilla

What you'll need

⅛ teaspoon salt

½ teaspoon pepper

1 tablespoon paprika

¼ teaspoon ground cayenne pepper

1 teaspoon garlic powder

1 teaspoon onion powder

1 tablespoon canola oil

1 pound boneless, skinless chicken breasts, cubed

1 large fresh yellow onion, chopped fine

3 fresh cloves garlic, chopped fine

1 large green bell pepper, chopped fine

8 whole wheat flour tortillas

1 cup shredded 2% cheddar cheese

½ cup light sour cream

What to do

1. In small bowl, blend salt, pepper, paprika, cayenne pepper, garlic powder, and onion powder. Rub chicken with spice mixture and set aside.

2. In large skillet heated to medium high, add oil. When oil is hot, add chicken, onion, garlic, and bell pepper. Cook until vegetables are sautéed and chicken is no longer pink, about 8 minutes. Remove from skillet and keep warm.

3. In same skillet heated to medium high, add 1 tortilla, top with 2 tablespoons cheddar cheese, and ⅛ chicken mixture, and fold in half. Brown both sides for 2 minutes a side or until golden brown.

4. Repeat with remaining tortillas.

5. Top tortillas with sour cream, if desired.

*Serving suggestion: Cut into wedges for appetizers.

Nutrition facts

(per serving)

Calories: 266

Total fat: 7 grams

Sodium: 501 mg

Carbohydrate: 31 grams

Fiber: 4 grams

Protein: 21 grams

Cost: $$

Spicy Chicken Tacos

Prep time: 15 minutes / Cook time: 20 minutes / Makes: 4 servings / Serving size: 2 tacos

What you'll need

8 small corn tortillas

1 pound boneless, skinless chicken breast, cut into 1-inch strips

⅛ teaspoon salt

¼ teaspoon ground black pepper

1 teaspoon onion powder

1 teaspoon garlic powder

2 teaspoons canola oil, divided

1 large yellow onion, sliced thin

1 green bell pepper, sliced thin

1 yellow bell pepper, sliced thin

1 jalapeño pepper, chopped

3 cloves garlic, minced

1 teaspoon ground cumin

Juice from one lime

½ cup chunky salsa

¼ cup fresh cilantro, chopped

¼ cup fresh green onions, chopped

Extra salsa for garnish, if desired

What to do

1. Preheat oven to 350 degrees. Wrap tortillas in foil and bake for about 7 minutes or until heated thoroughly.

2. Season chicken with salt, pepper, onion powder, and garlic powder. Warm 1 teaspoon oil in large skillet over medium-high heat. Add chicken and cook for about 7 minutes or until chicken is no longer pink. Transfer chicken to bowl and set aside.

3. Add remaining oil to pan and add onion, peppers, jalapeño, garlic, and cumin. Cook for about 5 minutes or until vegetables are crisp-tender.

4. Stir in lime juice, salsa, and cooked chicken.

5. Remove from heat and spoon mixture evenly into 8 tortillas, topping with cilantro, green onions, and salsa, if desired.

Nutrition facts
(per serving)

Calories: 285

Total fat: 5 grams

Sodium: 276 mg

Carbohydrate: 31 grams

Fiber: 5 grams

Protein: 30 grams

Cost: $$$

Spicy Noodles

Prep time: 15 minutes / Cook time: 25 minutes / Makes: 8 servings / Serving size: ⅛ mixture

What you'll need

½ pound button mushrooms

8 ounces boneless, skinless chicken breasts

3 tablespoons sesame oil

2 tablespoons low-sodium soy sauce

⅓ cup green onions, thinly sliced

¼ cup fresh ginger, peeled and thinly sliced

3 cloves garlic, minced

1 pinch red pepper flakes

1 teaspoon onion powder

1 teaspoon garlic powder

¾ pound whole wheat spaghetti, cooked

¼ teaspoon freshly ground black pepper

1 pound fresh baby spinach, washed and dried

What to do

1. Coat large skillet with nonstick cooking spray and heat over medium-high heat. Add mushrooms and sauté for 3 to 5 minutes, until they are browned. Remove from heat and keep warm.

2. Spray pan again and sauté chicken breasts over medium-high heat for about 6 minutes on each side. Remove from heat and, when cool enough to handle, shred.

3. Warm sesame oil and soy sauce in skillet over medium heat. Add green onions, ginger slices, garlic, red pepper, onion powder, and garlic powder, and cook until fragrant, about 2 minutes. Add noodles to skillet and toss well. Add freshly ground pepper and adjust seasoning to your taste.

4. Arrange spinach leaves on plate or in bowl. Add noodles and top with mushrooms and chicken.

Nutrition facts (per serving)

Calories: 154 / Total fat: 6 grams / Sodium: 199 mg / Carbohydrate: 16 grams
Fiber: 4 grams / Protein: 12 grams / Cost: $$

Spicy Tomato Soup

Prep time: 15 minutes / Cook time: 20 minutes / Makes: 4 cups / Serving size: 1 cup

What you'll need

1 (16 ounce) package frozen mixed bell pepper strips

1 (14.5 ounce) can no-salt-added diced tomatoes, undrained

1 (14.5 ounce) can fat-free, low-sodium chicken broth

1 (15.5 ounce) can no-salt-added navy beans, rinsed and drained

1 teaspoon dried parsley

1 tablespoon balsamic vinegar

½ teaspoon dried oregano

2 cloves garlic, chopped

¼ teaspoon crushed red pepper

1 tablespoon dried basil leaves

1 teaspoon garlic powder

1 teaspoon onion powder

⅛ teaspoon salt

1 tablespoon olive oil

What to do

1. In food processor, puree bell peppers, undrained tomatoes, broth, beans, parsley, vinegar, oregano, garlic, crushed red pepper, basil, garlic powder, and onion powder until slightly chunky.

2. Pour into large saucepan. Bring to boil over high heat. Reduce heat and simmer, cover for 20 minutes or until flavors are blended.

3. Remove from heat and stir in salt and oil.

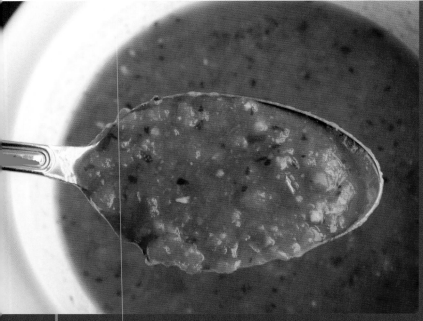

Nutrition facts
(per serving)

Calories: 237

Total fat: 3.5 grams

Sodium: 115 mg

Carbohydrate: 38 grams

Fiber: 14 grams

Protein: 13 grams

Cost: $

*

Spinach Quiche

Prep time: 10 minutes / Cook time: 45 minutes / Makes: 8 slices / Serving size: 1 slice

What you'll need

2 tablespoons light butter

4 cloves garlic, chopped

1 cup fresh mushrooms, chopped

1 cup yellow onion, chopped

1 (10 ounce) package frozen chopped spinach, thawed and drained

1 (6 ounce) package low-fat herb and garlic feta, crumbled

1 (8 ounce) package low-fat shredded cheddar cheese, divided

1 (9 inch) unbaked deep dish piecrust or 36 mini crusts

1 egg, beaten

4 egg whites, beaten

1 cup skim milk

1 teaspoon onion powder

1 teaspoon garlic powder

⅛ teaspoon salt

¼ teaspoon pepper

What to do

1. Preheat oven to 375 degrees.

2. In medium skillet, melt butter over medium heat. Sauté garlic, mushrooms, and onion in butter until lightly browned, about 7 minutes. Stir in spinach, feta, and ½ cup cheddar cheese. Season with salt and pepper. Spoon mixture into piecrust.

3. In medium bowl, whisk together eggs and milk. Season with onion powder, garlic powder, salt, and pepper. Pour into pastry shell.

4. Sprinkle top with remaining cheddar cheese and bake for 45 minutes, until set in center. Allow to stand 10 minutes before serving.

Nutrition facts (per serving)

Calories: 266 / Total fat: 13 grams / Sodium: 442 mg / Carbohydrate: 21 grams
Fiber: 2 grams / Protein: 17 grams / Cost: $$ / *

Split Pea Soup with Kale and Smoked Turkey Sausage

Prep time: 10 minutes / Cook time: 40 minutes / Makes: 10 cups / Serving size: 1 cup

What you'll need

1 tablespoon extra-virgin olive oil

1 large white onion, chopped

3 cloves garlic, chopped

2 large carrots, shredded

1 (1 pound) bag green split peas

4 cups low-sodium chicken broth

4 cups kale

1 teaspoon onion powder

1 teaspoon garlic powder

½ teaspoon ground black pepper

8 ounces smoked turkey sausage, sliced thin

What to do

1. Warm large saucepan to medium high. Add olive oil and warm for 30 seconds. Add onion, garlic, and carrots. Sauté for about 3 minutes. Add split peas and broth.

2. Bring mixture to boil, then turn heat to medium low and simmer for about 30 minutes.

3. Puree mixture in blender or food processor. Return to saucepan.

4. Bring mixture back to boil and add kale, all seasonings, and turkey sausage.

5. Adjust heat to medium and cook for about 10 minutes or until kale is cooked to desired tenderness.

6. Season to taste.

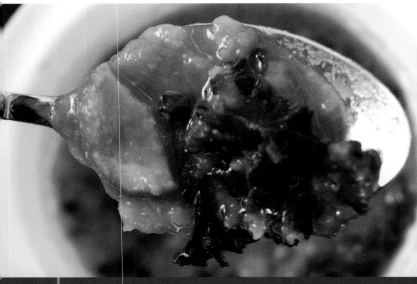

Nutrition facts
(per serving)

Calories: 253

Total fat: 5 grams

Sodium: 207 mg

Carbohydrate: 34 grams

Fiber: 13 grams

Protein: 20 grams

Cost: $$

*

Summer Spaghetti

Prep time: 15 minutes / Cook time: 12 minutes / Makes: 6 servings / Serving Size: ⅙ mixture

What you'll need

2 tablespoons extra-virgin olive oil

1 cup onion, chopped

1 tablespoon fresh garlic, chopped

1 cup yellow squash, sliced

1 cup zucchini, sliced

1 cup fresh button mushrooms, sliced

⅛ teaspoon salt

½ teaspoon fresh ground black pepper

½ teaspoon onion powder

½ teaspoon garlic powder

2 cups cooked whole wheat spaghetti noodles

1 cup cherry tomatoes, halved

What to do

1. Warm large, nonstick skillet to medium high. Add oil, onion, garlic, squash, zucchini, mushrooms, salt, black pepper, onion powder, and garlic powder. Simmer for 10 minutes or until vegetables are tender.

2. Add cooked pasta and tomatoes to skillet and cook an additional 2 minutes or until pasta and tomatoes are warm.

Nutrition facts (per serving)

Calories: 123 / Total fat: 5 grams / Sodium: 57 mg / Carbohydrate: 18 grams
Fiber: 3 grams / Protein: 4 grams / Cost: $$

Give us grateful hearts, our Father, for all Your mercies—

and make us mindful of the needs of others. Through Jesus Christ,

our Lord, we pray. Amen.

Tabbouleh

Prep time: 20 minutes / Chill time: 30 minutes / Makes: 8 servings / Serving size: ½ cup

What you'll need

3 cups cooked couscous

2 tablespoons extra-virgin olive oil

¼ cup fresh parsley, finely chopped

2 large tomatoes, chopped

½ cup green onions, finely chopped

1 large cucumber, peeled and chopped

2 tablespoons fresh mint, finely chopped

Juice and zest from 1 lemon

2 garlic cloves, minced

⅛ teaspoon salt

¼ teaspoon black pepper

What to do

1. Mix all ingredients in large mixing bowl.

2. Refrigerate for 30 minutes before serving.

Nutrition facts
(per serving)

Calories: 114

Total fat: 4 grams

Sodium: 44 mg

Carbohydrate: 18 grams

Fiber: 2 grams

Protein: 3 grams

Cost: $$

Taco Soup

Prep time: 15 minutes / Cook time: 30 minutes / Makes: 12 cups / Serving size: 1 cup

What you'll need

Soup:

1 pound lean ground turkey

1 cup onions, chopped

3 cloves garlic, chopped

5 cups low-sodium chicken broth

1 (15 ounce) can black beans

1 (15 ounce) can pinto beans

1 (15 ounce) can no-salt-added whole kernel corn, drained

1 (15 ounce) can diced tomatoes with green chilies

2 (15 ounce) cans diced tomatoes with oregano and basil

1 (4 ounce) can green chilies, diced

1 (4 ounce) can black olives, sliced and drained

2 teaspoons cumin

1 teaspoon onion powder

½ teaspoon salt

½ teaspoon black pepper

1 teaspoon garlic powder

1 teaspoon chili powder

1 teaspoon paprika

1 teaspoon oregano

Topping:

1 cup grated low-fat cheddar cheese

1 cup green onions, chopped

What to do

1. Warm large skillet to medium high; add cooking spray, ground turkey, onions, and garlic. Cook on medium-high heat until turkey is no longer pink and onions are soft; drain.

2. Transfer meat mixture to large stockpot. Place remaining ingredients in stockpot and cook for 30 minutes on medium-low heat, stirring occasionally.

3. Ladle into bowls and garnish each bowl with shredded low-fat cheese and chopped green onions.

Nutrition facts (per serving)

Calories: 208 / Total fat: 5 grams / Sodium: 433 mg / Carbohydrate: 25 grams
Fiber: 7 grams / Protein: 17 grams / Cost: $$$ / *

Tilapia Tacos with Corn Salsa

Prep time: 10 minutes / Cook time: 6 minutes / Makes: 6 servings / Serving size: 1 taco

What you'll need

1 cup no-salt-added canned corn kernels

½ cup red onion, diced

1 cup peeled, chopped jicama

1 cup red bell pepper, diced

1 cup fresh cilantro leaves, finely chopped

2 limes, zested and juiced

1 teaspoon cayenne pepper

1 teaspoon cumin

1 teaspoon onion powder

1 teaspoon garlic powder

1 tablespoon paprika

1 teaspoon ground black pepper

2 tablespoons olive oil

6 (4 ounce) fillets tilapia

6 whole wheat tortillas, warmed

What to do

1. Preheat grill for high heat.

2. In medium bowl, mix corn, red onion, jicama, red bell pepper, and cilantro. Stir in lime juice and zest.

3. In small bowl, combine seasonings. Brush each fillet with olive oil and sprinkle with spices.

4. Arrange fillets on grill grate and cook for 3 minutes per side. For each taco, top tortillas with fish, sour cream, and corn salsa.

Nutrition facts
(per serving)

Calories: 333

Total fat: 8 grams

Sodium: 398 mg

Carbohydrate: 39 grams

Fiber: 5 grams

Protein: 28 grams

Cost: $$

Tomato Florentine Soup

Prep time: 15 minutes / Cook time: 20 minutes / Makes: 8 cups / Serving size: 1 cup

What you'll need

2½ tablespoons olive oil

¼ cup onion, minced

1 tablespoon garlic, minced

3 tablespoons flour

4 cups low-sodium chicken stock

1 (15 ounce) can diced tomatoes

2 (8 ounce) cans tomato sauce

1 (10 ounce) package chopped spinach, thawed and squeezed dry

1 teaspoon dried basil

1 tablespoon sugar

⅛ teaspoon salt

¼ teaspoon black pepper

½ cup fat-free half-and-half

1 cup orzo pasta

What to do

1. In large sauce pot, heat oil and sauté onion and garlic. Add flour and stir. Add chicken stock and stir.

2. Add diced tomatoes, tomato sauce, spinach, and basil.

3. Simmer on low for about 15 minutes or until thickened.

4. Season with sugar, salt, and pepper to taste. Stir in half-and-half.

5. Add orzo pasta; let mixture set off heat for 20 minutes.

*Note: Final step may be skipped if you cook the pasta ahead of time.

Nutrition facts (per serving)

Calories: 161 / Total fat: 6 grams / Sodium: 129 mg / Carbohydrate: 22 grams
Fiber: 3 grams / Protein: 7 grams / Cost: $ / *

Dinner Recipes

Asian Baked Salmon

Prep time: 10 minutes / Cook time: 15 minutes / Makes: 6 servings / Serving size: 5 ounces

What you'll need

2 tablespoons Dijon mustard

3 tablespoons low-sodium soy sauce

2 teaspoons garlic, minced

2 tablespoons extra-virgin olive oil

2 teaspoons ginger, minced

1 teaspoon garlic powder

1 teaspoon onion powder

½ teaspoon ground black pepper

2 pounds fresh salmon

What to do

1. In small bowl, combine and stir all ingredients except salmon.

2. Preheat oven to 400 degrees. Coat large cookie sheet with cooking spray.

3. Place salmon, skin side down on cookie sheet. Brush salmon with mustard sauce.

4. Bake salmon for 15 minutes or until fish flakes easily with fork.

Nutrition facts
(per serving)

Calories: 262

Total fat: 14 grams

Saturated fat: 2 grams

Sodium: 390 mg

Carbohydrate: 1.5 grams

Fiber: 0 grams

Protein: 30 grams

Cost: $$$

Baked Chimichangas

Prep time: 30 minutes / Cook time: 15 minutes / Makes: 6 chimichangas / Serving size: 1 chiminchanga

What you'll need

1 onion, chopped

3 cups shredded cooked chicken breast

2 cups low-sodium salsa, divided

1 tablespoon cumin

1 tablespoon chili powder

6 large (10 inch) whole wheat flour tortillas

1 cup reduced-fat cheddar cheese

½ cup low-sodium chicken broth

¼ teaspoon ground black pepper

¼ cup flour

½ cup fat-free half-and-half

1 (4 ounce) can green chilies, chopped

What to do

1. Preheat oven to 425 degrees.

2. In nonstick skillet, sauté onion in cooking spray over medium-high heat for about 4 minutes. Add chicken, 1½ cups salsa, cumin, and chili powder. Heat for about 3 minutes.

3. Place ⅙ mixture down center of each tortilla; top with ⅙ of shredded cheese.

4. Fold sides and ends over filling and roll up.

5. Place seam side down in 9x13-inch baking dish coated with cooking spray. Bake uncovered for 15 minutes.

6. Meanwhile, in small saucepan heat broth and pepper over medium heat. Combine flour and half-and-half in small bowl until smooth. Stir into broth. Bring to boil and cook for 2 minutes or until thick. Stir in chilies.

7. Spoon sauce over top. Garnish with additional ½ cup salsa.

Nutrition facts (per serving)

Calories: 446 / Total fat: 10 grams / Saturated fat: 5 grams / Sodium: 558 mg
Carbohydrate: 52 grams / Fiber: 6 grams / Protein: 36 grams / Cost: $$

Bean Bolognese

Prep time: 20 minutes / Cook time: 20 minutes / Makes: 4 cups pasta and 3 cups sauce /
Serving size: 1 cup pasta and ¾ cup sauce (1 cup cooked pasta = 2 ounces)

What you'll need

8 ounces whole wheat
   fettuccini

1 (14 ounce) can of salad
   beans*

2 tablespoons olive oil

1 small onion, chopped

½ cup carrot, chopped

¼ cup celery, chopped

4 cloves garlic, chopped

1 bay leaf

½ cup low-sodium chicken
   broth

1 tablespoon tomato paste

1 (14 ounce) can diced
   tomatoes, low-sodium

¼ cup parsley, chopped

1 cup raw spinach, packed

8 ounces whole-wheat
   fettuccini

¼ cup Parmesan cheese,
   shredded

*Salad beans are a mixture of chickpeas, kidney beans, and pinto beans. If you can't find this, you can substitute your favorite kind of bean. Substituting beans for ground beef in this recipe cuts fat by one-third and saturated fat by 80 percent.

What to do

1. Boil water in large pot. Cook pasta until just tender, about 9 minutes or according to package directions. Drain.
2. Mash ½ cup beans with fork in small bowl.
3. Warm oil in medium saucepan over medium heat. Add onion, carrots, and celery. Cook until softened, about 10 minutes.
4. Add garlic and bay leaf; cook, stirring, until fragrant, about 15 seconds.
5. Add broth and tomato paste; increase heat to high and boil until most of liquid evaporates, 3 to 4 minutes.
6. Add tomatoes and their juices, 2 tablespoons parsley, mashed beans, and spinach. Bring to lively simmer and cook, stirring occasionally, until thickened, about 6 minutes.
7. Add remaining whole beans; cook, stirring occasionally, until heated through, 1 to 2 minutes more.
8. Divide pasta among 4 bowls. Discard bay leaf and top pasta with sauce; sprinkle each bowl with 1 tablespoon Parmesan and remaining parsley.

Nutrition facts (per serving)

Calories: 412 / Total fat: 11 grams / Saturated fat: 2 grams / Sodium: 414 mg
Carbohydrate: 69 grams / Fiber: 13 grams / Protein: 13 grams / Cost: $

Beef and Macaroni

Prep time: 15 minutes / Cook time: 65 minutes / Makes: 8 servings / Serving size: ⅛ mixture

What you'll need

2 pounds 90% lean ground beef

2 cups onions, chopped

3 cloves garlic, chopped

4 cups water

30 ounces no-salt-added tomato sauce

30 ounces no-salt-added diced tomatoes

1 tablespoon Italian seasoning

1 teaspoon garlic powder

1 teaspoon onion powder

⅛ teaspoon of salt

1 teaspoon dried basil

½ teaspoon ground black pepper

1 teaspoon dried oregano

2 bay leaves

2 tablespoons light soy sauce

2 cups dried whole wheat elbow macaroni

What to do

1. In large stockpot, brown ground beef, onions, and garlic over medium heat, cooking until meat is no longer pink. Drain off all fat and return meat to stockpot.

2. Add water, tomato sauce, tomatoes, all seasonings, and soy sauce. Cover and let cook for 20 minutes on medium heat.

3. Add macaroni; cover and simmer over medium-low heat for an additional 20 minutes. Turn heat off, remove bay leaves, and allow mixture to thicken for 10 to 15 minutes before serving.

Nutrition facts
(per serving)

Calories: 372

Total fat: 12 grams

Saturated fat: 5 grams

Sodium: 245 mg

Carbohydrate: 38 grams

Fiber: 6 grams

Protein: 29 grams

Cost: $$

*

Beef Lasagna

Prep time: 10 minutes / Cook time: 30 minutes / Makes: 12 servings (12 squares) / Serving size: 1 square

What you'll need

½ pound lean ground sirloin

½ pound turkey sausage

3 garlic cloves, minced

½ cup onion, diced

30 ounces no-salt-added tomato sauce

1 (14 ounce) can no-salt-added diced tomatoes

1 teaspoon dried basil

1 teaspoon dried oregano

⅛ teaspoon salt

¼ teaspoon ground black pepper

¼ teaspoon red pepper flakes

1 teaspoon sugar

1 egg

1 cup light ricotta cheese

1 tablespoon dried parsley

8 ounces mozzarella cheese, part skim, shredded

4 ounces cheddar cheese, low-fat, shredded

10 ounces whole wheat lasagna noodles, cooked (about 12 sheets)

What to do

1. Preheat oven to 375 degrees. Coat large (2 quart) glass casserole dish with cooking spray; set aside.

2. Add cooking spray to large saucepan heated to medium high; add ground sirloin, sausage, garlic, and onions. Cook for about 7 minutes or until meat is no longer pink and onions are soft. Drain and return to pan.

3. Add tomato sauce, diced tomatoes, basil, oregano, salt, pepper, red pepper flakes, and sugar to drained meat. Simmer for 8 minutes on low heat, stirring occasionally; set aside.

4. In medium mixing bowl, stir egg and ricotta cheese together; add parsley, 1 cup mozzarella cheese, and all cheddar cheese; set aside.

5. Place 4 layers of noodles in prepared casserole dish. Place ⅓ of cheese mixture on noodles, followed by ⅓ of meat mixture; repeat procedure 2 more times. Top casserole with remaining cup of mozzarella cheese.

6. Cover with foil and bake in preheated oven for 30 minutes.

Nutrition facts (per serving)

Calories: 291 / Total fat: 10 grams / Saturated fat: 5 grams / Sodium: 351 mg
Carbohydrate: 28 grams / Fiber: 6 grams / Protein: 21 grams / Cost: $$$ / *

Beef and Mushroom Stroganoff

Prep time: 15 minutes / Cook time: 50 minutes / Makes: 6 servings / Serving size: ⅙ mixture

What you'll need

1 tablespoon extra-virgin olive oil

1 cup onion, chopped

1 tablespoon garlic, minced

2 cups button mushrooms, freshly sliced

1 teaspoon onion powder

1 teaspoon garlic powder

1 teaspoon dried thyme leaves

⅛ teaspoon salt

¼ teaspoon ground black pepper

1 pound beef top sirloin, thinly sliced

1½ cups low-sodium beef broth

1 (8 ounce) package uncooked egg noodles

½ cup half-and-half

½ cup light sour cream

What to do

1. Place olive oil in large, nonstick skillet over medium-high heat. Add onion, garlic, and mushrooms. Cook until onions and mushrooms are tender, about 10 minutes. Stir in onion powder, garlic powder, thyme, salt, and pepper.

2. Place sirloin in skillet and cook meat until browned evenly, about 5 minutes.

3. Stir beef broth into skillet. Let mixture simmer for about 20 minutes.

4. Meanwhile, boil noodles for about 8 minutes; drain and set aside.

5. Pour half-and-half and sour cream into meat mixture. Simmer for about 5 minutes. Serve over cooked noodles.

Nutrition facts (per serving)

Calories: 394 / Total fat: 18 grams / Saturated fat: 7 grams / Sodium: 271 mg
Carbohydrate: 33 grams / Fiber: 2 grams / Protein: 25 grams / Cost: $$

Beef Tenderloin with Mushroom Sauce

Prep time: 10 minutes / Cook time: 15 minutes / Makes: 6 servings / Serving size: 1 steak with ⅙ sauce mixture

What you'll need

4 tablespoons light butter, divided

½ cup onion, chopped

3 cloves garlic, chopped

2 cups fresh mushrooms, sliced

1 green onion, minced fine

1 tablespoon Worcestershire sauce

⅛ teaspoon salt

1 pound beef tenderloin

1 tablespoon salt-free steak seasoning

What to do

1. Melt 3 tablespoons of butter in large skillet heated to medium high. Add onions, garlic, mushrooms, green onion, Worcestershire sauce, and salt. Simmer for about 7 minutes, or until mushrooms are cooked down. Place mushrooms in bowl and set aside.

2. Cut beef tenderloin into 6 rounds; season with salt-free steak seasoning.

3. Melt remaining butter into same skillet; heat to medium high.

4. Place steak onto skillet and cook for 4 minutes on each side; turn only one time, making sure a nice crust develops on both sides of steaks.

5. Pour equal parts of mushroom sauce on each steak.

Nutrition facts
(per serving)

Calories: 237

Total fat: 17 grams

Saturated fat: 8 grams

Sodium: 86 mg

Carbohydrate: 3 grams

Fiber: 0 grams

Protein: 16 grams

Cost: $$$$

Broccoli Beef with Rice

Prep time: 20 minutes / Cook time: 22 minutes / Makes: 4 servings / Serving size: 3 ounces beef, ½ cup vegetable mixture, ½ cup rice

What you'll need

12 ounces round steak, fat trimmed, thinly sliced

1 tablespoon light soy sauce

¼ teaspoon ground black pepper

1 teaspoon sesame oil

1 tablespoon cornstarch

2 tablespoons olive oil, divided

1 pound fresh broccoli, thinly sliced

1 medium onion, chopped

¼ cup water

3 cloves garlic, minced

2 cups cooked brown rice

What to do

1. Marinate beef with soy sauce, pepper, sesame oil, and cornstarch for 10 minutes.
2. In large skillet, warm 1 tablespoon olive oil over medium-high heat. Add broccoli, onion and water. Stir well and cook for 5 minutes.
3. Remove from skillet and set on plate or large bowl.
4. Heat remaining tablespoon olive oil in same skillet. Add beef and garlic and cook beef until no longer pink, about 6 minutes, stirring occasionally. Return broccoli to pan to reheat.
5. Serve broccoli and beef mixture over brown rice.

Nutrition facts
(per serving)

Calories: 367

Total fat: 14 grams

Saturated fat: 3 grams

Sodium: 219 mg

Carbohydrate: 37 grams

Fiber: 5 grams

Protein: 24 grams

Cost: $$

Cashew-Crusted Tilapia with Mango Salsa

Prep time: 10 minutes / Cook time: 6 minutes / Makes: 4 servings / Serving size: 1 fish fillet with ½ cup salsa

What you'll need

1 large mango, chopped

1 large tomato, seeded and chopped

¼ cup yellow onion, chopped fine

¼ cup fresh cilantro, chopped fine

1 lime, juiced and zested

⅛ teaspoon salt

Pepper to taste

3 egg whites

¼ cup cashews, crushed fine

¼ cup yellow cornmeal

4 (4 ounce) tilapia fillets

1 teaspoon olive oil

1 teaspoon light butter

What to do

1. In medium bowl, combine mango, tomato, onion, cilantro, lime juice, lime zest, salt, and pepper; set aside.

2. Place egg whites in bowl. Mix cashews and cornmeal in another bowl.

3. Dip each fish fillet in egg whites, then cashew mixture. Place coated fish on clean plate.

4. Heat large, nonstick skillet to medium high. Add olive oil and butter. Cook fish for about 3 minutes on each side.

5. Serve with mango salsa on top.

Nutrition facts (per serving)

Calories: 258 / Total fat: 9 grams / Saturated fat: 2 grams / Sodium: 131 mg
Carbohydrate: 20 grams / Fiber: 3 grams / Protein: 28 grams / Cost: $$

Ever-present God, we witness Your creative presence in each and every meal. Help us to share that witness with others. Amen.

Chicken and Rice Bowl with Teriyaki Glaze

Prep time: 20 minutes / Cook time: 20 minutes / Makes: 6 servings / Serving size: ⅔ cup chicken mixture with ⅓ cup cooked rice

What you'll need

2 teaspoons olive oil

1 tablespoon fresh ginger, chopped

1 tablespoon fresh garlic, chopped

½ cup yellow onions, chopped

1 cup shredded carrots

1 cup red bell pepper, chopped

1 cup yellow bell pepper, chopped

1 pound boneless, skinless chicken breast, cut into 1-inch cubes

2 cups frozen edamame, shelled

2 tablespoons reduced-sodium soy sauce

1 tablespoon reduced-sodium teriyaki sauce

1 tablespoon honey

1 teaspoon sesame oil

½ teaspoon cornstarch

¼ cup green onions, chopped

1 tablespoon sesame seeds, toasted

2 cups cooked hot brown rice

What to do

1. Heat oil in large, nonstick skillet to medium high. Add ginger, garlic, yellow onions, carrots, and bell peppers. Sauté for 5 minutes.

2. Add chicken cubes and sauté an additional 5 minutes.

3. Add edamame and sauté for 2 minutes.

4. Meanwhile, in small bowl, whisk soy sauce, teriyaki sauce, honey, sesame oil, cornstarch, and green onions.

5. Add sauce mixture to chicken mixture; stir to combine. Cook for an additional 5 minutes, stirring occasionally.

6. Toss in toasted sesame seeds.

7. Serve mixture over hot brown rice.

Nutrition facts (per serving)

Calories: 254/ Total fat: 5 grams / Saturated fat: 1 gram / Sodium: 327 mg
Carbohydrate: 31 grams / Fiber: 5 grams / Protein: 22 grams / Cost: $$

Chicken and Rice Casserole

Prep time: 20 minutes / Cook time: 90 minutes / Makes: 12 servings / Serving size: 1 chicken breast with 1 cup rice mixture

What you'll need

2 tablespoons olive oil, divided

12 (4 ounce) boneless, skinless chicken breasts

4 garlic cloves, minced

1 cup onion, chopped

3 cups brown rice

1 cup dry white cooking wine

3 cups no-salt-added chicken broth

1 tablespoon dried rubbed sage

1 teaspoon dried basil

1 tablespoon dried thyme

⅛ teaspoon salt

2½ cups frozen green peas

½ teaspoon freshly ground pepper

2 cups plum tomato, diced

12 ounces artichoke hearts, chopped

¾ cup bottled roasted red bell peppers, thinly sliced into strips

What to do

1. Over medium heat, warm 1 tablespoon oil in large skillet. Add chicken and garlic; cook 5 minutes on each side or until lightly browned. Remove from pan. Set aside; keep warm. Preheat oven to 400 degrees.

2. Over medium heat, warm 1 tablespoon oil in large skillet. Add onion and rice; sauté 15 minutes or until rice is lightly browned. Add broth and next 6 ingredients; bring to boil. Top with peas, tomato, and artichokes. Stir well.

3. Bake rice mixture, uncovered, at 400 degrees for 50 minutes; stir after 25 minutes. Place chicken atop rice mixture. Cover and cook 15 minutes or until liquid is absorbed. Stir well; top with pepper strips.

Nutrition facts
(per serving)

Calories: 388
Total fat: 6 grams
Saturated fat: 1 gram
Sodium: 272 mg
Carbohydrate: 49 grams
Fiber: 6 grams
Protein: 34 grams
Cost: $$$

Chicken, Mushroom, and Spinach Crepes with Bacon

Prep time: 20 minutes / Cook time: 60 minutes / Makes: 8 crepes / Serving size: 1 crepe

What you'll need

Crepes:
½ cup whole wheat flour
½ cup flour
2 eggs
1 cup skim milk
⅛ teaspoon salt
2 tablespoons light butter, melted

Filling:
2 cups chicken breasts, cooked and shredded
16 ounces frozen spinach, drained, rinsed, and squeezed dry
1 teaspoon onion powder
1 teaspoon garlic powder
½ teaspoon ground black pepper
1 ounce turkey bacon, cooked and crumbled

6 ounces part skim mozzarella cheese, shredded
1 tablespoon olive oil
2 cups button mushrooms, sliced
3 cloves garlic, minced
1 tablespoon light butter
¼ cup flour
2 cups skim milk
¼ cup Parmesan cheese, shredded

What to do

1. For crepes: Whisk flours and eggs. Gradually add milk; stir well.
2. Add salt and butter; beat until smooth.
3. Heat nonstick skillet to medium high; coat with cooking spray. Pour or scoop batter onto skillet, using about ¼ cup for each crepe. You should be able to make 8 crepes.
4. Cook crepe for 2 minutes or until bottom is brown. Flip and cook other side. Set crepes aside and prepare filling.
5. For filling: Heat oven to 375 degrees.
6. Place chicken, spinach, onion powder, garlic powder, pepper, and bacon in large bowl along with half mozzarella cheese.
7. Heat large, nonstick skillet to medium high and add olive oil. Add mushrooms and garlic; sauté for about 6 minutes or until mushrooms are cooked to desired tenderness.
8. Add mushrooms to chicken mixture.
9. In separate saucepan heated to medium, melt butter. Add flour and cook for 1 minute. Gradually stir in milk and Parmesan cheese. Cook until thickened, about 5 minutes, stirring constantly. Add a little over half of mixture to chicken mixture.
10. Divide overall mixture evenly into 8 prepared crepes.
11. Roll up crepes and place in large glass baking dish coated with cooking spray.
12. Top with remaining white sauce and remaining mozzarella cheese.
13. Cover with foil and bake for 30 minutes or until crepes are heated through.

Nutrition facts (per serving)

Calories: 261 / Total fat: 13 grams / Saturated fat: 6 grams / Sodium: 381 mg
Carbohydrate: 12 grams / Fiber: 2 grams / Protein: 26 grams / Cost: $$

Chicken and Mushroom Casserole with Wild Rice

Prep time: 20 minutes / Cook time: 90 minutes / Makes: 8 servings / Serving size: ⅛ casserole, about 1½ cups

What you'll need

2 cups water
½ cup wild rice
2 pounds boneless, skinless chicken breast
2 tablespoons extra-virgin olive oil, divided
⅛ teaspoon salt
¼ teaspoon ground black pepper
2 leeks, chopped and rinsed

1 cup onion, chopped
½ cup celery, chopped
3 cloves garlic, minced
2 pounds mushrooms, sliced
¾ cup low-sodium chicken broth
¼ cup flour
2 cups skim milk
½ cup Parmesan cheese, shredded

½ cup light sour cream
¼ cup parsley, chopped
1 teaspoon onion powder
1 teaspoon garlic powder
2 cups frozen French-cut green beans
1 cup water chestnuts, sliced thin
½ cup almonds, sliced

What to do

1. Combine water and rice in small saucepan; bring to boil. Cover, reduce heat, and simmer until tender, about 35 minutes. Drain.
2. Preheat oven to 350 degrees. Place chicken breasts on foil-lined cookie sheet coated with cooking spray. Sprinkle 1 tablespoon olive oil, salt, and pepper over chicken breast. Rub chicken until coated. Cook chicken in preheated oven for about 15 minutes, slice thin, and set aside.
3. Warm remaining olive oil in large skillet over medium heat. Add leeks, onion, celery, and garlic. Cook for about 3 minutes. Add mushrooms and cook for about 10 minutes, stirring occasionally.
4. Add chicken broth and increase heat to high; cook until most of liquid has been evaporated, about 5 minutes. Sprinkle vegetables with flour and stir well. Add skim milk and bring to boil for 1 minute. Stir in Parmesan, sour cream, parsley, onion powder, and garlic powder. Remove from heat.
5. Coat 9x13-inch baking dish with cooking spray.
6. Place chicken in large bowl. Add mushroom mixture, cooked rice, green beans, and water chestnuts.
7. Place mixture into prepared dish.
8. Sprinkle with almonds.
9. Bake in preheated oven for 30 minutes.

Nutrition facts (per serving)

Calories: 384 / Total fat: 13 grams / Saturated fat: 3 grams / Sodium: 363 mg
Carbohydrate: 30 grams / Fiber: 4 grams / Protein: 39 grams / Cost: $$$ / *

Chicken-Asparagus Stir-Fry

Prep time: 20 minutes / Cook time: 15 minutes / Makes: 4 servings / Serving size: 1 cup stir-fry plus ½ cup cooked rice

What you'll need

1 pound boneless, skinless chicken breast, cut into 1-inch cubes

2 tablespoons light soy sauce, divided

2 tablespoons sesame oil, divided

2 green onions, chopped

3 cloves garlic, chopped

2 pounds fresh asparagus

2 tablespoons sesame seeds

⅓ cup low-sodium chicken broth

2 teaspoons cornstarch

1 cup carrots, shredded

½ cup water chestnuts, thinly sliced

2 cups hot cooked brown rice

What to do

1. Combine chicken, 1 tablespoon soy sauce, 1 tablespoon sesame oil, green onions, and garlic in medium bowl, stirring to mix. Let stand.

2. Break off tough ends of asparagus and discard. Cut spears in 1-inch pieces.

3. In 12-inch stir-fry pan over medium-high heat, toast sesame seeds until light brown. Place seeds on paper towel.

4. In medium bowl, stir together broth, cornstarch, and remaining soy sauce until blended.

5. In stir-fry pan, combine remaining oil, asparagus, and carrots. Cook over medium-high heat, stirring frequently for 4 minutes. Place asparagus mixture into bowl containing chicken broth mixture.

6. Raise heat to high and add chicken pieces and liquid to skillet. Cook for 6 minutes or until chicken is no longer pink.

7. Return reserved asparagus and broth mixture to skillet. Continue cooking until asparagus and carrots are hot and liquid is thickened, about 5 minutes.

8. Sprinkle dish with toasted sesame seeds and water chestnuts.

9. Serve over hot cooked brown rice.

Nutrition facts (per serving)

Calories: 394 / Total fat: 12 grams / Saturated fat: 2 grams / Sodium: 365 mg
Carbohydrate: 40 grams / Fiber: 8 grams / Protein: 35 grams / Cost: $$

Chicken Curry

Prep time: 20 minutes / Cook time: 20 minutes / Makes: 4 servings / Serving size: 1 cup chicken with ½ cup rice

What you'll need

4 cups sliced Swiss chard

1 cup water

1 pound skinned, boned chicken breast halves, cut crosswise into thin slices

1 tablespoon cornstarch

1 tablespoon olive oil

1 cup onion, diced

1⅓ cups fat-free, low-sodium chicken broth

1 cup baby carrots, sliced

½ cup light coconut milk

1 tablespoon tomato paste

2 teaspoons ground cumin

2 teaspoons curry powder

⅛ teaspoon salt

¼ teaspoon ground red pepper

2 cups cooked brown rice

- -

What to do

1. In medium covered saucepan, steam chard in water, 2 minutes or until crisp-tender; drain.

2. Combine chicken and cornstarch in small bowl.

3. Warm oil in large, nonstick skillet over medium-high heat.

4. Add onion; stir-fry 2 minutes. Stir in chicken, and cook 6 minutes or until browned.

5. Stir in broth and next 7 ingredients (through red pepper); reduce heat to medium. Cook 5 minutes, stirring often.

6. Add Swiss chard, and cook 2 minutes.

7. Serve with rice.

Nutrition facts
(per serving)

Calories: 352

Total fat: 10 grams

Saturated fat: 4 grams

Sodium: 241 mg

Carbohydrate: 35 grams

Fiber: 5 grams

Protein: 32 grams

Cost: $$

Chicken Sausage with Tomatoes and Capers over Polenta

Prep time: 15 minutes / Cook time: 20 minutes / Makes: 6 servings / Serving size: ½ cup polenta and ⅙ chicken sausage mixture

What you'll need

2½ cups water

1¼ cup low-sodium chicken broth, divided

1 cup plain white cornmeal

⅛ teaspoon salt

⅓ cup grated Parmesan cheese

1 tablespoon olive oil

6 ounces chicken sausage, sliced thin

2 cups mushrooms, sliced thin

1 cup onions, diced

3 cloves garlic, chopped

1 can (15 ounces) no-salt-added, fire-roasted tomatoes

¼ cup capers, drained

1 tablespoon dried basil leaves

Dash red pepper flakes (optional)

What to do

1. Mix first 4 ingredients in medium saucepan. Place over medium-high heat, stirring constantly until mixture boils and thickens, about 5 minutes.

2. Add Parmesan cheese; stir until melted. Cover pan and keep warm over low heat, stirring occasionally.

3. In large skillet, heat oil over medium-high heat. Add sausage and cook until brown, about 5 minutes. Place sausage on plate and keep warm. Add mushrooms, onions, and garlic to same skillet and cook for about 5 minutes on medium-high heat. Stir in tomatoes, remaining ¼ cup chicken broth, capers, basil, and red pepper. Simmer for about 5 minutes.

4. Add sausage to skillet and heat thoroughly.

5. To serve, spoon about ½ cup polenta into 6 bowls, top with sausage mixture and sprinkling of Parmesan cheese.

Nutrition facts (per serving)

Calories: 188 / Total fat: 7 grams / Saturated fat: 2 grams / Sodium: 478 mg
Carbohydrate: 24 grams / Fiber: 3 grams / Protein: 8 grams / Cost: $$

Chickpea and Spinach Soup with Shrimp

Prep time: 10 minutes / Cook time: 30 minutes / Makes: 10 cups / Serving size: 1⅓ cups

What you'll need

2 tablespoons olive oil, divided

2 onions, coarsely chopped (about 2½ cups)

6 cloves garlic, finely minced

1 small potato, peeled and sliced

3 cups canned chickpeas, rinsed and drained, divided

5 cups reduced-sodium chicken stock

½ teaspoon of onion powder

¼ teaspoon freshly ground black pepper

½ teaspoon garlic powder

6 cups fresh spinach, cut into thin strips and well washed

1 ounce (about 22) almonds, coarsely chopped

1 pound cooked shrimp, shelled and deveined

What to do

1. In large saucepan, warm 1 tablespoon olive oil over medium heat. Add chopped onions and cook for 10 to 15 minutes or until translucent. Add garlic and stir for 1 to 2 minutes. Then add sliced potato, half the chickpeas, and chicken broth; bring to boil.

2. Simmer and cook until potatoes and beans are falling apart, about 20 minutes. Puree soup in blender. Season with onion powder, pepper, and garlic powder. Just before serving, bring soup to simmer. In large sauté pan, heat 2 teaspoons of oil and wilt spinach. Add pureed soup. Stir in remaining whole cooked chickpeas.

3. In small sauté pan, over medium heat, warm 1 teaspoon of oil. Sauté almonds for 3 minutes and add to soup. Finally, add cooked shrimp.

Nutrition facts
(per serving)
Calories: 229
Total fat: 7 grams
Saturated fat: 2 grams
Sodium: 335 mg
Carbohydrate: 27 grams
Fiber: 5 grams
Protein: 17 grams
Cost: $$$
*

Chili

Prep time: 15 minutes / Cook time: 35 minutes / Makes: 10 servings / Serving size: 1 cup

What you'll need

1 pound ground turkey

1 tablespoon olive oil

1 yellow onion, chopped

1 green bell pepper, chopped

3 cloves garlic, chopped

1 cup frozen corn, thawed

1 teaspoon onion powder

1 teaspoon garlic powder

½ teaspoon salt

¼ teaspoon pepper

⅛ teaspoon cayenne pepper

2 tablespoons chili powder

1 can (15 ounce) no-salt-added crushed tomatoes

1 can (15 ounce) no-salt-added tomato sauce

½ cup water

1 can red beans, rinsed and drained

1 can black beans, rinsed and drained

What to do

1. Preheat large skillet to medium-high. Coat with cooking spray.

2. Add turkey and cook until no longer pink, about 6 minutes. Drain and set aside.

3. In large, nonstick skillet, heat olive oil. Add onion, pepper, garlic, corn, and seasonings. Cook 6 minutes or until vegetables are softened.

4. Add remaining ingredients and cooked turkey. Simmer for 20 to 25 minutes.

5. Add more water if thinner consistency is desired.

Nutrition facts
(per serving)

Calories: 231

Total fat: 6 grams

Saturated fat: 1 gram

Sodium: 461 mg

Carbohydrate: 30 grams

Fiber: 9 grams

Protein: 16 grams

Cost: $$

*

Coconut Tilapia

Prep time: 5 minutes / Cook time: 12 minutes / Makes: 4 fillets / Serving size: 1 fillet

What you'll need

Tilapia:

1 ounce (about ¾ cup) unsweetened flaked coconut, chopped

2 tablespoons flour

⅛ teaspoon ground black pepper

¼ teaspoon garlic powder

2 teaspoons reduced-sodium Creole seasoning

4 (4 ounce) tilapia fillets

½ cup cornstarch

4 ounces egg substitute

Sauce:

½ cup sugar-free apricot preserves

1 tablespoon whole grain mustard

What to do

1. Preheat oven to 350 degrees. Coat large cookie sheet with cooking spray; set aside.

2. In medium mixing bowl, blend coconut, flour, pepper, garlic powder, and Creole seasoning. In separate bowl, toss tilapia fillets in cornstarch and shake off. Dip fillet in egg substitute, then roll in coconut mixture. Place fillet onto prepared cookie sheet, repeating process for remaining tilapia fillets.

3. Bake in preheated oven for about 12 minutes or until fish flakes easily with fork.

4. For sauce, combine preserves and mustard.

5. Serve tilapia warm with apricot sauce for dipping.

Nutrition facts (per serving)

Calories: 190 / Total fat: 6 grams / Saturated fat: 4 grams / Sodium: 312 mg
Carbohydrate: 30 grams / Fiber: 2 grams / Protein: 10 grams / Cost: $

Corn Chowder

Prep time: 15 minutes / Cook time: 45 minutes / Makes: 8 servings / Serving size: about 1 cup

What you'll need

4 cups corn, cut from cob (about 8 large ears), divided

1 tablespoon olive oil

2 cups onion, chopped

1 cup celery, diced

4 cloves garlic, minced

2 cups baking potato (about 1¼ pounds), peeled and diced

2 (10.5 ounce) cans low-sodium chicken broth

¼ cup plus 2 tablespoons flour

⅛ teaspoon salt

¼ teaspoon black pepper

⅛ teaspoon ground red pepper

2 cups skim milk

1 teaspoon Worcestershire sauce

What to do

1. Position knife blade in food processor bowl; add 2½ cups corn. Process until smooth; set aside. Add oil to a large saucepan over medium heat. Add onion, celery, and garlic; sauté 10 minutes or until vegetables are tender, stirring occasionally. Add potato and broth; bring to boil.

2. Reduce heat and simmer for 15 minutes or until potato is tender, stirring often. Add corn puree and remaining 1½ cups corn; cook 8 minutes. Combine water and rice in a small saucepan; bring to a boil. Cover, reduce heat and simmer until tender, about 35 minutes. Drain.

3. In small bowl, gradually add milk and Worcestershire sauce, blending with wire whisk; add to chowder. Cook over medium heat 10 minutes or until thickened, stirring constantly.

Nutrition facts (per serving)

Calories: 188 / Total fat: 3 grams / Saturated fat: 0.5 grams / Sodium: 194 mg
Carbohydrate: 36 grams / Fiber: 5 grams / Protein: 8 grams / Cost: $$ / *

Corn Bread Casserole

Prep time: 15 minutes / Cook time: 35 minutes / Makes: 10 servings / Serving size: ¹/₁₀ mixture

What you'll need

2 cups self-rising cornmeal, plus additional for dusting pan

1 pound lean turkey

1 teaspoon onion powder

1 teaspoon garlic powder

¼ teaspoon pepper

½ cup egg substitute

1 (15 ounce) can cream-style corn

1 cup skim milk

¼ cup canola oil

1 medium onion, chopped

¼ cup jalapeño peppers, finely chopped

8 ounces low-fat, extra-sharp cheddar cheese, grated

What to do

1. Preheat oven to 375 degrees. Grease 9x13-inch baking pan with cooking spray and sprinkle with cornmeal.

2. In large skillet over medium-high heat, brown turkey, breaking it up with spoon until crumbled. Drain off fat from meat. Season meat with onion powder, garlic powder, and pepper.

3. In large bowl, combine cornmeal, egg substitute, corn, milk, and oil. Spread half of corn bread batter over bottom of prepared pan and sprinkle evenly with meat. Layer onion, peppers, and cheese on top. Cover with remaining batter.

4. Bake casserole until top is golden brown, about 35 minutes. Let cool before cutting.

Nutrition facts (per serving)

Calories: 330 / Total fat: 12 grams / Saturated fat: 3 grams / Sodium: 271 mg
Carbohydrate: 37 grams / Fiber: 2 grams / Protein: 19 grams / Cost: $$ / *

Gracious and merciful God, join me in enjoying this meal.

Please nourish within me a new love for You. Amen.

Fettuccine Alfredo with Shrimp, Broccoli, and Red Bell Peppers

Prep time: 5 minutes / Cook time: 10 minutes / Makes: 6 servings / Serving size: ⅙ mixture

What you'll need

½ pound whole wheat fettuccini pasta

1 tablespoon olive oil

1 cup mushrooms, sliced

3 cups fresh broccoli florets, sliced

1 red bell pepper, sliced

3 cloves garlic, chopped fine

½ cup half-and-half

½ cup fat-free half-and-half

¼ cup fresh parsley, chopped

½ cup shredded Parmesan cheese

1 pound cooked shrimp, peeled and deveined

⅛ teaspoon salt

¼ teaspoon ground black pepper

What to do

1. Cook pasta according to package directions; set aside.

2. In large, nonstick skillet, warm oil over medium heat. Add mushrooms, broccoli, bell pepper, and garlic. Cook for about 5 minutes or until vegetables are of desired tenderness, stirring frequently.

3. Add half-and-half, fat-free half-and-half, parsley, and Parmesan cheese. Cook until sauce is thickened, about 5 minutes. Stir in cooked shrimp, pepper, and salt and heat thoroughly.

4. Pour mixture over hot cooked fettuccine noodles.

Nutrition facts
(per serving)

Calories: 341

Total fat: 10 grams

Saturated fat: 4 grams

Sodium: 261 mg

Carbohydrate: 40 grams

Fiber: 5 grams

Protein: 23 grams

Cost: $$$

Garlic and Shrimp Penne with Spinach and Cherry Tomatoes

Prep time: 15 minutes / Cook time: 12 minutes / Makes: 12 servings / Serving size: 1/12 mixture

What you'll need

3 tablespoons extra-virgin olive oil

1 cup onions, chopped

3 cloves garlic, chopped

2 tablespoons white wine

1 (10 ounce) package fresh baby spinach leaves

1 cup cherry tomatoes, quartered

1/8 teaspoon salt

1/4 teaspoon ground black pepper

1 pound cooked shrimp, deveined and peeled

1/2 teaspoon crushed red pepper flakes

12 ounces whole wheat penne pasta, cooked according to package directions

2 tablespoons shredded Parmesan cheese

What to do

1. Warm large, nonstick skillet to medium-high heat. Add oil, onions, and garlic, heating until onions begin to soften, about 3 minutes. Add white wine, spinach, and cherry tomatoes. Season with salt and pepper. Cook for an additional 5 minutes.

2. Stir in cooked shrimp and crushed red pepper flakes and sauté for 3 minutes.

3. Toss in pasta and Parmesan cheese. Heat thoroughly.

Nutrition facts (per serving)

Calories: 186 / Total fat: 5 grams / Saturated fat: 1 gram / Sodium: 125 mg
Carbohydrate: 25 grams / Fiber: 4 grams / Protein: 11 grams / Cost: $$$

Grilled Tilapia with Strawberry-Avocado Salsa

Prep time: 15 minutes / Cook time: 10 minutes / Makes: 4 servings / Serving size: 1 tilapia fillet and ¼ cup salsa

What you'll need

Fish:

¼ cup olive oil

1 clove garlic, minced

2 teaspoons dried basil

2 teaspoons black pepper

¼ teaspoon salt

4 (4 ounce) tilapia fillets

Salsa:

½ cup strawberries, chopped

½ cup peaches, chopped

¼ cup avocado, chopped and peeled

2 tablespoons red onion, finely chopped

2 tablespoons fresh cilantro, chopped

½ teaspoon grated lime

2 tablespoons fresh lime juice

2 teaspoons seeded jalapeño pepper, finely chopped

¼ teaspoon sugar

What to do

1. Preheat grill to medium high.

2. Mix olive oil, garlic, basil, pepper, and salt in bowl.

3. Dip both sides of fish into mixture.

4. Wrap each fillet in piece of aluminum foil.

5. Cook fillets on grill, 3 to 4 minutes each side.

6. Make sure flesh is white and flaky before taking fish off grill.

7. For salsa, combine all ingredients in medium bowl and toss gently.

8. Pour salsa on top of tilapia.

Nutrition facts (per serving)

Calories: 262 / Total fat: 17 grams / Saturated fat: 3 grams / Sodium: 206 mg
Carbohydrate: 6 grams / Fiber: 2 grams / Protein: 23 grams / Cost: $$

Herbed Chicken and Dumplings

Prep time: 20 minutes / Cook time: 1 hour / Makes: 2 servings / Serving size: about 2 cups

What you'll need

6 ounces skinless, boneless chicken thighs, cut into bite-sized pieces

¾ cup celery, finely diced

1 cup carrot, finely chopped

1 cup onion, finely chopped

¼ teaspoon dried thyme

5 parsley sprigs

2 bay leaves

3 cups fat-free, low-sodium chicken broth

¼ cup flour

¼ cup whole wheat pastry flour (or whole wheat flour or white whole wheat flour)

2 tablespoons fresh parsley, chopped

¼ teaspoon baking powder

¼ teaspoon salt

⅛ teaspoon pepper

¼ cup skim milk (add more if dough looks dry)

What to do

1. Warm large saucepan over medium-high heat. Coat pan with cooking spray. Add chicken to pan; cook 4 minutes, browning on all sides. Remove chicken from pan; keep warm.

2. Place celery and next 5 ingredients (through bay leaves) into pan; sauté 5 minutes or until onion is tender. Return chicken to pan; cook 1 minute.

3. Add broth to pan; bring mixture to boil. Cover, reduce heat, and simmer 30 minutes.

4. In separate medium bowl, combine flours, chopped parsley, baking powder, salt, and pepper. Add milk, stirring just until moist. Spoon by heaping teaspoonfuls into broth mixture; cover and simmer 10 minutes or until dumplings are done. Discard parsley sprigs and bay leaf.

Nutrition facts
(per serving)

Calories: 347
Total fat: 6 grams
Saturated fat: 2 grams
Sodium: 585 mg
Carbohydrate: 44 grams
Fiber: 5 grams
Protein: 30 grams
Cost: $
*

Indian Chicken Curry

Prep time: 20 minutes / Cook time: 20 minutes / Makes: 4 servings / Serving size: 1 cup chicken mixture with ½ cup rice

What you'll need

5 cups sliced Swiss chard

1 pound boneless, skinless chicken breast, sliced thin

1 tablespoon cornstarch

1 tablespoon extra-virgin olive oil

1 cup onion, diced

1⅓ cups fat-free, low-sodium chicken broth

1 cup baby carrots, sliced

½ cup light coconut milk

1 tablespoon no-salt-added tomato paste

2 teaspoons ground cumin

1 teaspoon curry powder

1 teaspoon cinnamon

⅛ teaspoon salt

Dash ground red pepper

2 cups cooked brown rice

1 ounce unsalted peanuts, chopped

What to do

1. Steam Swiss chard, covered, for about 5 minutes or until crisp-tender, drain and set aside.

2. Combine chicken and cornstarch in medium mixing bowl. Season with salt and pepper if desired.

3. Warm oil in large, nonstick skillet to medium-high heat. Add onion and chicken and cook for about 6 minutes or until chicken is no longer pink in center and onions are golden brown.

4. Stir in broth, carrots, milk, tomato paste, cumin, curry powder, cinnamon, salt, and red pepper.

5. Reduce heat to medium, cover and cook for 5 minutes, stirring occasionally.

6. Add Swiss chard and cook for 2 minutes.

7. Serve with rice and sprinkle each dish with peanuts.

Nutrition facts (per serving)

Calories: 389 / Total fat: 13 grams / Saturated fat: 4 grams / Sodium: 250 mg
Carbohydrate: 35 grams / Fiber: 6 grams / Protein: 34 grams / Cost: $$$ / *

Italian Meat Loaf

Prep time: 15 minutes / Cook time: 1 hour / Makes: 6 slices / Serving size: 1 slice

What you'll need

2 tablespoons extra-virgin olive oil
1 green bell pepper, diced
1 onion, diced
3 large cloves garlic, minced
½ pound ground sirloin
½ pound ground turkey sausage
2 egg whites

1 egg
3 ounces wheat bread crumbs
½ cup reduced-sodium Parmesan cheese, grated
1 tablespoon Worcestershire sauce
1 tablespoon balsamic vinegar
1 teaspoon crushed fennel seeds

1 teaspoon dried basil
1 teaspoon dried oregano
⅛ teaspoon salt
½ teaspoon ground black pepper
1 teaspoon onion powder
1 teaspoon garlic powder
1 cup low-sodium marinara sauce

What to do

1. Preheat oven to 350 degrees.

2. Warm oil in medium, nonstick skillet over medium-high heat. Add peppers, onion, and garlic. Sauté for about 4 minutes or until vegetables are soft.

3. Combine all remaining ingredients except marinara in large bowl. Add sautéed vegetables to this mixture.

4. Form meat into loaf. Place cookie rack on top of cookie sheet and put loaf atop cookie rack.

5. Top with marinara sauce.

6. Bake for 50 minutes or until an instant-read thermometer registers 160 degrees in middle of meat loaf.

7. Remove from oven; let rest for 10 minutes.

8. Slice and serve.

Nutrition facts
(per serving)
Calories: 323
Total fat: 16 grams
Saturated fat: 5 grams
Sodium: 510 mg
Carbohydrate: 18 grams
Fiber: 3 grams
Protein: 25 grams
Cost: $$
*

Jambalaya

Prep time: 20 minutes / Cook time: 30 minutes / Makes: 6 servings / Serving size: 1½ cups

What you'll need

½ pound smoked turkey kielbasa sausage, cut into 1-inch pieces

1 large onion, chopped

1 large green bell pepper, chopped

2 celery ribs, chopped

2 garlic cloves, minced

1 tablespoon canola oil

2 cans (14.5 ounce each) diced tomatoes, undrained

½ cup water

1 teaspoon dried thyme

¼ teaspoon salt

¼ teaspoon pepper

¼ teaspoon cayenne pepper

1 pound uncooked medium shrimp, peeled and deveined

2 cups cooked brown rice

What to do

1. In large saucepan, sauté sausage, onion, green pepper, celery, and garlic in oil for 8 minutes over medium-high heat. Add tomatoes, water, thyme, salt, pepper, and cayenne; bring to boil. Reduce heat; cover and simmer for 15 minutes.

2. Add shrimp; simmer 5 minutes longer or until shrimp turn pink. Stir in rice.

Nutrition facts
(per serving)

Calories: 276

Total fat: 8 grams

Saturated fat: 1 gram

Sodium: 587 mg

Carbohydrate: 28 grams

Fiber: 4 grams

Protein: 24 grams

Cost: $$$

Linguine with Portobello Mushrooms, Shrimp, and Broccoli

Prep time: 20 minutes / Cook time: 20 minutes / Makes: 4 servings / Serving size: 1½ cups

What you'll need

½ pound whole grain linguine

1 tablespoon olive oil

3 garlic cloves, chopped

1 pound raw shrimp, peeled and deveined

1 pound broccoli florets, cut into bite-sized pieces

2 portobello mushrooms, cut in half and sliced thin

¼ cup dry white wine

2 cans (14.5 ounce) no-salt-added diced tomatoes

2 teaspoons crushed red pepper flakes

1 teaspoon onion powder

1 teaspoon garlic powder

1 teaspoon dried oregano

⅛ teaspoon salt

½ cup fresh basil leaves, chopped

½ cup pasta water, reserved

¼ cup Parmesan cheese, grated

What to do

1. Bring large pot of lightly salted water to boil and cook pasta to al dente, according to package directions.

2. Meanwhile, heat oil in large, nonstick skillet. Add garlic and shrimp, cooking until shrimp is no longer pink. Transfer to metal bowl and keep warm. Add broccoli and mushrooms to skillet. Cook over high heat, stirring for 2 minutes, until mushrooms begin to wilt. Reduce heat to low and add wine, tomatoes, crushed red pepper flakes, onion powder, garlic powder, oregano, and salt. Cook, simmering slowly for 2 minutes, stirring twice. Add basil and stir.

3. Drain pasta, reserving ½ cup pasta water. Add water to sauce; increase heat and boil for 1 minute to reduce slightly.

4. Divide pasta among 4 plates. Top with sauce and sprinkle with cheese. Serve immediately.

Nutrition facts (per serving)

Calories: 474 / Total fat: 9 grams / Saturated fat: 2 grams / Sodium: 323 mg
Carbohydrate: 63 grams / Fiber: 9 grams / Protein: 35 grams / Cost: $$

Mexican Chicken Casserole

Prep time: 20 minutes / Cook time: 60 minutes / Makes: 8 servings / Serving size: 1 cup

What you'll need

4 cups fat-free, low-sodium chicken broth

1 (4 ounce) can green chilies, chopped

2 pounds skinned, boned chicken breasts

1 tablespoon olive oil

1 cup onion, chopped

1 cup fat-free evaporated milk

1 cup (4 ounces) shredded low-fat Monterey Jack cheese

¼ cup (2 ounces) low-fat cream cheese

1 (10 ounce) can enchilada sauce

12 (6 inch) corn tortillas

½ cup (2 ounces) shredded reduced-fat extra-sharp cheddar cheese

1 ounce baked tortilla chips, crushed (about 6 chips)

What to do

1. Preheat oven to 350 degrees.

2. Combine broth and chilies in large skillet; bring to boil.

3. Add chicken; reduce heat and simmer 15 minutes or until chicken is no longer pink, stirring occasionally.

4. Remove chicken from cooking liquid; cool chicken. Set aside cooking liquid.

5. Shred meat with two forks and set aside.

6. Warm oil in large, nonstick skillet over medium heat.

7. Add onion; sauté 3 minutes or until soft.

8. Add cooking liquid, milk, Monterey Jack, cream cheese, and enchilada sauce; stir well. Stir in shredded chicken. Cook 2 minutes; remove from heat.

9. Coat casserole dish with cooking spray.

10. Place 4 tortillas in bottom of casserole dish. Spoon 2 cups of chicken mixture over tortillas.

11. Repeat layers twice, ending with chicken mixture on top; sprinkle with cheddar cheese and chips.

12. Bake at 350 for 30 minutes or until well heated. Let stand 10 minutes before serving.

Nutrition facts (per serving)

Calories: 355 / Total fat: 8 grams / Saturated fat: 3 grams / Sodium: 659 mg
Carbohydrate: 32 grams / Fiber: 4 grams / Protein: 24 grams / Cost: $$$ / *

Orange Glazed Chicken with Almonds

Prep time: 10 minutes / Cook time: 30 minutes / Makes: 4 servings / Serving size: 1 piece of chicken with ¼ cup sauce

What you'll need

1 pound boneless, skinless chicken breasts

1 teaspoon onion powder

1 teaspoon garlic powder

¼ teaspoon ground black pepper

¼ cup orange juice concentrate, thawed, divided

1 teaspoon lemon zest

2 tablespoons freshly squeezed lemon juice

½ cup low-sodium chicken broth

2 teaspoons cornstarch

1 tablespoon sugar

1 tablespoon light butter

¼ cup green onions, chopped

2 tablespoons fresh parsley, chopped

¼ cup toasted slivered almonds

What to do

1. Preheat oven to 400 degrees. Place chicken breasts on foil-lined cookie sheet coated with cooking spray.

2. In small bowl, blend onion powder, garlic powder, black pepper, and 2 tablespoons orange juice. Brush mixture over both sides of chicken.

3. Bake for 20 minutes in preheated oven.

4. Mix remaining 2 tablespoons of orange juice, zest, lemon juice, chicken broth, cornstarch, and sugar. Place over medium-high heat and simmer for 10 minutes.

5. Remove from heat, whisk in butter, green onions, and parsley.

6. Pour sauce over chicken; top with almonds.

(per serving)
Calories: 215
Total fat: 7 grams
Saturated fat: 2 grams
Sodium: 85 mg
Carbohydrate: 8 grams
Fiber: 1 gram
Protein: 28 grams
Cost: $$
*

Oven-Fried Catfish

Prep time: 10 minutes / Cook time: 15 minutes / Makes: 4 servings / Serving size: 1 catfish fillet

What you'll need

¼ cup yellow cornmeal

¼ cup dry bread crumbs, whole wheat preferred

¼ teaspoon black pepper

2 teaspoons onion powder

2 teaspoons garlic powder

1 teaspoon paprika

4 (6 ounce) catfish fillets

½ cup skim milk

2 tablespoons light butter, melted

What to do

1. Preheat oven to 400 degrees.

2. Mix cornmeal, bread crumbs, pepper, onion powder, garlic powder, and paprika.

3. Dip fish in milk.

4. Coat with cornmeal mixture.

5. Place fish in baking pan coated with cooking spray.

6. Pour butter over fish.

7. Bake uncovered until fish flakes very easily with fork, about 15 minutes.

Nutrition facts (per serving)

Calories: 246 / Total fat: 7 grams / Saturated fat: 3 grams / Sodium: 147 mg
Carbohydrate: 14 grams / Fiber: 2 grams / Protein: 30 grams / Cost: $$

Creating God, help us to see the abundance of Your wonderful creation.

Open our eyes to new ways of enjoying the foods of Your world. Amen.

Oven-Fried Chicken

Prep time: 10 minutes / Cook time: 18 minutes / Makes: 6 servings / Serving size: 1 chicken breast

What you'll need

½ cup cornmeal

½ cup panko bread crumbs

1 teaspoon dried tarragon

1 teaspoon dried basil

1 teaspoon dried oregano

¼ teaspoon salt

¼ teaspoon ground black pepper

¼ teaspoon ground red pepper

1 teaspoon onion powder

1 teaspoon garlic powder

4 egg whites

¼ cup low-fat buttermilk

½ cup white whole wheat flour, sifted

6 (4 ounce) boneless, skinless chicken breasts

What to do

1. Preheat oven to 375 degrees.

2. In shallow pan, combine first 10 ingredients.

3. In another shallow pan, combine egg whites and milk.

4. In third shallow pan, place flour.

5. Coat chicken with flour, dip in egg mixture, then roll in cornmeal mixture.

6. Place coated chicken in large glass baking dish coated with cooking spray.

7. Bake uncovered for 18 minutes or until chicken is no longer pink in center and juices run clear.

Nutrition facts
(per serving)

Calories: 240

Total fat: 2 grams

Saturated fat: 1 gram

Sodium: 267 mg

Carbohydrate: 22 grams

Fiber: 3 grams

Protein: 32 grams

Cost: $$

Pasta with Peas, Red Peppers, and Pesto

Prep time: 20 minutes / Cook time: 12 minutes / Makes: 8 servings / Serving size: 1½ cups

What you'll need

2 large red bell peppers

5 tablespoons olive oil, divided

1 cup fresh basil leaves, washed and dried

1 cup fresh spinach, washed and dried

1 ounce pine nuts

2 garlic cloves

¼ cup shredded Parmesan cheese

⅛ teaspoon salt

¼ teaspoon ground black pepper

1 (16 ounce) package whole wheat penne pasta, cooked according to package directions

1 cup frozen peas, thawed

What to do

1. Preheat oven to 450 degrees.

2. Place whole bell peppers on foil-lined cookie sheet and brush peppers with 1 tablespoon olive oil. Place peppers in preheated oven for 7 minutes or until peppers begin to blacken. Remove from oven and place peppers in gallon zip-top bag; set aside.

3. Meanwhile, combine basil, spinach, pine nuts, garlic, and Parmesan cheese in food processor and blend until smooth. Stream in remaining olive oil. Season with salt and pepper; blend until smooth.

4. Remove bell peppers from bag; slice peppers in half and remove skin, seeds, and inner membranes. Cut into thin strips; set aside.

5. Warm large skillet over medium-high heat; coat with cooking spray.

6. Combine cooked pasta, thawed peas, sliced bell peppers, and prepared pesto sauce; cook for 5 minutes or until all ingredients are heated through.

Nutrition facts (per serving)

Calories: 337 / Total fat: 13 grams / Saturated fat: 2 grams / Sodium: 75 mg
Carbohydrate: 50 grams / Fiber: 8 grams / Protein: 7 grams / Cost: $$$ / *

Penne Pasta with Italian Spinach

Prep time: 15 minutes / Cook time: 15 minutes / Makes: 8 servings / Serving size: 1½ cups

What you'll need

4 tablespoons olive oil, divided

40 ounces frozen spinach, thawed, rinsed, and squeezed of excess moisture

3 cloves garlic, minced

¼ cup Parmesan cheese, shredded

6 large tomatoes, chopped

⅛ teaspoon salt

¼ teaspoon ground black pepper

1 (16 ounce) box whole wheat penne pasta, cooked according to package directions

What to do

1. Put 2 tablespoons oil in large skillet over medium-high heat. Add spinach, garlic, and Parmesan cheese. Cook for 5 minutes; stir in tomatoes and cook an additional 3 minutes.

2. Add salt and pepper.

3. Toss pasta into spinach mixture and pour remaining olive oil over.

4. Serve warm.

Nutrition facts
(per serving)

Calories: 329

Total fat: 10 grams

Saturated fat: 2 grams

Sodium: 161 mg

Carbohydrate: 55 grams

Fiber: 12 grams

Protein: 11 grams

Cost: $$

Pizza Lasagna

Prep time: 20 minutes / Cook time: 35 minutes / Makes: 12 servings (12 squares) / Serving size: 1 square

What you'll need

2 (29 ounce) cans no-salt-added diced tomatoes

1 large onion, diced

1 large green bell pepper, diced

¼ teaspoon black pepper

2 teaspoons oregano

2 teaspoons basil

1 teaspoon thyme

2 teaspoons garlic powder

2 teaspoons onion powder

1 pound Italian turkey sausage

1 cup turkey pepperoni

1 (16 ounce) box lasagna noodles, cooked according to package directions

2 cups 2% shredded mozzarella cheese

½ cup Parmesan cheese, grated

What to do

1. Preheat oven to 400 degrees.

2. In saucepan, combine first 9 ingredients; simmer on low heat for 10 minutes. Let cool and puree mixture in food processor; set aside.

3. Meanwhile, over medium-high heat, cook and crumble turkey sausage in nonstick skillet coated with cooking spray; set aside.

4. In separate pan warmed to medium-high heat, add turkey pepperoni and cook for 5 minutes or until crispy; set aside.

5. Coat large glass baking dish with cooking spray. Add 3 tablespoons of sauce to bottom of dish and add layer of noodles. Top noodles with layer of sauce, layer of both meats, and layer of mozzarella cheese; repeat procedure until all ingredients are used, for total of four layers. Top with Parmesan cheese.

6. Cover dish with foil and bake for 35 minutes. Remove foil and continue baking for 5 more minutes or until cheese is golden brown. Let stand for 15 minutes before cutting.

Nutrition facts (per serving)

Calories: 311 / Total fat: 10 grams / Saturated fat: 4 grams / Sodium: 518 mg
Carbohydrate: 38 grams / Fiber: 6 grams / Protein: 20 grams / Cost: $$ / *

Red and Green Pepper Steak with Rice

Prep time: 20 minutes / Cook time: 20 minutes / Makes: 4 servings / Serving size: ¼ pepper mixture and ½ cup rice

What you'll need

1 pound sirloin steak, trimmed and cut into thin strips

1 teaspoon onion powder

1 teaspoon garlic powder

1 green bell pepper, sliced

1 red bell pepper, sliced

1 large yellow onion, sliced

4 cloves garlic, minced

2 tablespoons reduced-sodium soy sauce

½ teaspoon ground black pepper

½ cup low-sodium beef broth

1 tablespoon cornstarch

1 (28 ounce) can no-salt-added whole tomatoes

2 cups cooked brown rice

What to do

1. Season steak with onion powder and garlic power. Warm large, nonstick skillet on medium-high heat. Coat with cooking spray.

2. Add seasoned meat. Cook until meat is no longer pink, about 6 minutes. Transfer meat to bowl and keep warm. In same skillet, add peppers, onion, and garlic. Sauté vegetables for about 5 minutes or until vegetables are tender.

3. Meanwhile, in small bowl, whisk soy sauce, black pepper, beef broth, and cornstarch. Add this mixture to pepper mixture. Return cooked steak to skillet. Add can of whole tomatoes, breaking up tomatoes with wooden spoon.

4. Let mixture simmer for about 5 minutes.

5. Serve over hot cooked rice.

Nutrition facts
(per serving)

Calories: 395
Total fat: 10 grams
Saturated fat: 3 grams
Sodium: 398 mg
Carbohydrate: 40 grams
Fiber: 6 grams
Protein: 36 grams
Cost: $$$
*

Red Beans and Rice

Prep time: 15 minutes / Cook time: 12 minutes / Makes: 6 servings / Serving size: ⅙ mixture

What you'll need

2 tablespoons extra-virgin olive oil

1 onion, chopped

1 cup bell pepper, chopped

1 cup celery, chopped

5 cloves garlic, chopped

¼ cup fresh parsley, chopped

1 teaspoon dried thyme

Dash salt

1 teaspoon hot and spicy salt-free seasoning

½ teaspoon ground black pepper

1 teaspoon onion powder

1 teaspoon garlic powder

2 (15 ounce) cans cooked red beans, rinsed and drained (or dried red beans, cooked)

2 cups cooked brown rice

3 dashes hot sauce

What to do

1. Warm large, nonstick skillet to medium-high heat. Add oil, onion, bell pepper, celery, and garlic, heating until vegetables begin to soften, about 7 minutes.

2. Season vegetables with all seasonings (parsley through garlic powder).

3. Add beans to skillet and heat thoroughly.

4. Add rice to skillet and season with hot sauce.

Nutrition facts
(per serving)

Calories: 253

Total fat: 6 grams

Saturated fat: 1 gram

Sodium: 396 mg

Carbohydrate: 44 grams

Fiber: 10 grams

Protein: 10 grams

Cost: $

*

Roasted Vegetable Lasagna

Prep time: 40 minutes / Cook time: 35 minutes / Makes: 12 servings (12 squares) / Serving size: 1 square

What you'll need

2 large eggplants, peeled and sliced into 1-inch rounds

5 summer squashes, sliced into 1-inch rounds

1 cup button mushrooms, sliced

1 large yellow onion, chopped

4 cloves garlic, minced

3 cups no-salt-added tomato sauce

¼ teaspoon black pepper

½ teaspoon oregano

½ teaspoon basil

½ teaspoon thyme

1 teaspoon garlic powder

1 teaspoon onion powder

1 (16 ounce) box lasagna noodles, cooked according to package directions

½ cup Italian-style bread crumbs

2 cups 2% shredded mozzarella cheese

½ cup grated Parmesan cheese

What to do

1. Preheat oven to 400 degrees.

2. Sprinkle eggplant with salt and let drain in colander for 15 minutes. Rinse eggplant and pat dry. Arrange eggplant in single layer on baking sheet along with squash, mushrooms, onion, and garlic. Roast vegetables in preheated oven for 35 minutes.

3. Meanwhile, in medium saucepan warmed to medium-high heat, add tomato sauce and seasonings; simmer for 5 minutes or until sauce is thickened and bubbly, stirring occasionally.

4. Coat large glass baking dish with thin layer of tomato sauce. Line dish with single layer of lasagna noodles. Spread ⅓ of roasted vegetables over noodles and sprinkle with a few tablespoons of bread crumbs. Pour ½ cup sauce over vegetables and sprinkle with ½ cup mozzarella cheese.

5. Repeat procedure 2 more times.

6. Finish with final layer of noodles and remaining sauce. Sprinkle remaining mozzarella cheese and Parmesan cheese on top.

7. Lower oven temperature to 350 degrees. Cover dish with foil and bake for 35 minutes. Remove foil and continue baking for 5 more minutes or until cheese is golden brown.

8. Let stand for 15 minutes before cutting.

Nutrition facts (per serving)

Calories: 280 / Total fat: 6 grams / Saturated fat: 3 grams / Sodium: 198 mg
Carbohydrate: 47 grams / Fiber: 10 grams / Protein: 12 grams / Cost: $$$$ / *

Seared Trout over Succotash

Prep time: 10 minutes / Cook time: 25 minutes / Makes: 4 servings / Serving size: 1 fillet with 1 cup succotash

What you'll need

Fish:

2 tablespoons olive oil

1 teaspoon paprika

⅛ teaspoon salt

¼ teaspoon ground black pepper

1 teaspoon onion powder

1 teaspoon garlic powder

1 teaspoon spicy salt-free seasoning

4 (6 ounce) boneless trout fillets

Succotash:

2 tablespoons light butter

1 small onion, chopped

1 cup red bell peppers, chopped

1 cup frozen lima beans, thawed

1 cup fresh or frozen corn, thawed

1 cup fat-free half-and-half

2 tablespoons flour

1 teaspoon onion powder

1 teaspoon garlic powder

⅛ teaspoon salt

¼ teaspoon ground black pepper

1 cup low-sodium chicken broth

¼ cup fresh parsley

What to do

1. For fish: In large, nonstick skillet, warm oil over medium-high heat. In small mixing bowl, stir paprika, salt, black pepper, onion powder, garlic powder, and salt-free seasoning.

2. Season trout evenly with seasonings.

3. Place fillets in skillet and cook for 3 minutes on each side or until fish flakes easily with fork. Set aside and keep warm.

4. For succotash: Warm butter in large skillet over medium heat. Add onion and red bell pepper and cook for 3 minutes. Add beans, corn, half-and-half, flour, onion powder, garlic powder, salt, and pepper.

5. Bring to simmer and cook for 5 minutes. Add broth and cook an additional 5 minutes.

6. Distribute succotash evenly among 4 plates and place fish on top. Garnish with fresh parsley.

Nutrition facts (per serving)

Calories: 454 / Total fat: 17 grams / Saturated fat: 5 grams / Sodium: 204 mg
Carbohydrate: 33 grams / Fiber: 5 grams / Protein: 43 grams / Cost: $$

Shepherd's Pie

Prep time: 15 minutes / Cook time: 33 minutes / Makes: 4 servings / Serving size: ¼ casserole

What you'll need

- 1 (10 ounce) bag frozen cauliflower florets
- 4 ounces reduced-fat cream cheese
- ¼ cup skim milk
- 2 teaspoons garlic powder
- 2 teaspoons onion powder
- 1 pound ground turkey
- 1 teaspoon extra-virgin olive oil
- 1 teaspoon salt-free herbed seasoning
- 2 carrots, peeled and chopped
- 1 large onion, chopped
- 1 clove garlic, chopped
- 2 tablespoons light butter
- 2 tablespoons flour
- 1 cup low-sodium beef stock or broth
- 1 tablespoon Worcestershire sauce
- 1 cup frozen peas
- 1 teaspoon sweet paprika
- 2 tablespoons fresh parsley leaves, chopped

What to do

1. Place cauliflower in bowl, cover with plastic wrap, and microwave until tender, 8 to 10 minutes. Drain and place in food processor with cream cheese, milk, garlic powder, and onion powder. Process until smooth; set aside.
2. Warm large skillet over medium-high heat. Add oil to hot pan with ground turkey.
3. Season meat with salt-free herbed seasoning. Brown and crumble meat for 3 to 4 minutes.
4. Add chopped carrot, onion, and garlic to meat. Cook vegetables with meat 5 minutes, stirring frequently.
5. In second small skillet over medium heat, cook light butter and flour together for 2 minutes.
6. Whisk in beef broth and Worcestershire sauce. Thicken gravy 1 minute. Add gravy to meat and vegetables. Stir in peas.
7. Preheat broiler to high.
8. Fill small rectangular casserole with meat and vegetable mixture. Spoon cauliflower mixture evenly over meat. Sprinkle top with paprika.
9. Broil 6 to 8 inches from heat until cauliflower is evenly browned. (Note: Watch cauliflower closely, as it can burn quickly.) Top casserole dish with chopped parsley and serve.

Nutrition facts (per serving)

Calories: 371 / Total fat: 18 grams / Saturated fat: 7 grams / Sodium: 395 mg
Carbohydrate: 24 grams / Fiber: 5 grams / Protein: 29 grams / Cost: $$ / *

Shrimp Creole

Prep time: 10 minutes / Cook time: 10 minutes / Makes: 4 servings / Serving size: 1½ cups

What you'll need

1 (14 ounce) can no-salt-added diced tomatoes

1 cup low-sodium chili sauce

1 large bell pepper, chopped

1 cup celery, chopped

1 small onion, chopped

4 cloves garlic, minced

1 teaspoon dried basil

1 teaspoon dried oregano

1 teaspoon garlic powder

1 teaspoon onion powder

1 teaspoon dried parsley

1 teaspoon hot and spicy salt-free seasoning

⅛ teaspoon salt

¼ teaspoon ground black pepper

1 pound large shrimp, raw, peeled and deveined

2 cups brown rice, cooked

What to do

1. Coat skillet with cooking spray. Combine tomatoes, chili sauce, bell pepper, celery, onion, garlic, and all seasonings in skillet. Bring to boil and cook for 2 minutes.

2. Turn heat to medium and simmer for 8 minutes.

3. Add shrimp and cook an additional 3 minutes or until shrimp are heated through.

4. Serve over hot cooked brown rice.

Nutrition facts
(per serving)

Calories: 339

Total fat: 3 grams

Saturated fat: 0 grams

Sodium: 241 mg

Carbohydrate: 52 grams

Fiber: 5 grams

Protein: 14 grams

Cost: $$

*

Shrimp Étouffée

Prep time: 30 minutes / Cook time: 20 minutes / Makes: 4 servings / Serving size: ¼ mixture

What you'll need

3 tablespoons light butter

1 cup green bell pepper, chopped

1 cup onion, chopped

1 cup celery, chopped

3 cloves garlic, minced

1 tablespoon flour

1 (14 ounce) can no-salt-added diced tomatoes

1 teaspoon dried basil

1 teaspoon dried oregano

1 teaspoon garlic powder

1 teaspoon onion powder

1 teaspoon dried parsley

½ teaspoon ground red pepper

1 teaspoon hot and spicy salt-free seasoning

1 pound large raw shrimp, peeled and deveined

2 cups brown rice, cooked

What to do

1. Coat skillet with cooking spray; melt butter. Add green bell pepper, onion, celery, and garlic. Sauté for about 5 minutes over medium-high heat. Add flour and cook for 1 minute.

2. Stir in tomatoes and all seasonings.

3. Cook, stirring occasionally for about 8 minutes. Stir in shrimp, simmer for 3 minutes or until shrimp are thoroughly cooked.

4. Serve over hot cooked brown rice.

Nutrition facts (per serving)

Calories: 380 / Total fat: 7 grams / Saturated fat: 3 grams / Sodium: 244 mg
Carbohydrate: 54 grams / Fiber: 5 grams / Protein: 29 grams / Cost: $$

Most precious Father, as we enjoy this meal, let us not forget

those who are hungry; while we share in fellowship with one another,

let us not forget those who are lonely. Amen.

Shrimp Scampi

Prep time: 15 minutes / Cook time: 15 minutes / Makes: 6 servings / Serving size: 1 cup

What you'll need

12 ounces whole wheat linguine

2 tablespoons light butter

2 tablespoons extra-virgin olive oil

1 tablespoon garlic, minced

2 cups mushrooms, sliced thin

1 red bell pepper, sliced thin

1 pound large raw shrimp, peeled and deveined

⅛ teaspoon salt

½ teaspoon black pepper

1 teaspoon onion powder

1 teaspoon garlic powder

¼ cup fresh parsley, chopped

1 lemon, juiced and zested

What to do

1. Cook pasta according to package directions; set aside.

2. Melt butter and oil in large skillet over medium heat. Add garlic, mushrooms, and red bell pepper and cook for about 3 minutes. Add shrimp. Season with salt, pepper, onion powder, garlic powder, parsley, and lemon juice and zest. Cook for 3 minutes or until shrimp are cooked thoroughly.

3. Add linguine and toss to combine.

Nutrition facts (per serving)

Calories: 351 / Total fat: 9 grams / Saturated fat: 2 grams / Sodium: 133 mg
Carbohydrate: 49 grams / Fiber: 7 grams / Protein: 20 grams / Cost: $$$

Shrimp with Rice and Black Bean Salsa

Prep time: 15 minutes / Cook time: 10 minutes / Makes: 4 servings / Serving size: 1 cup salsa, ½ cup rice, 4 ounces shrimp

What you'll need

2 cups cooked black beans

1 cup fresh corn kernels

½ cup red onion, finely diced

1 jalapeño pepper, finely diced

1 cup cherry tomatoes, halved

1 lime, juiced

2 tablespoons olive oil, divided

Dash salt

1 tablespoon olive oil

1 pound raw shrimp

⅛ teaspoon salt

¼ teaspoon ground black pepper

1 teaspoon onion powder

1 teaspoon garlic powder

½ teaspoon ground red pepper

2 cups cooked brown rice, kept warm

What to do

1. In large bowl, combine first 8 ingredients; toss well, let set at room temperature until ready to serve.
2. For shrimp, warm olive oil in nonstick skillet over medium-high heat.
3. Toss shrimp with all seasonings and add to pan.
4. Cook for about 3 minutes or until shrimp is pink.
5. Divide rice evenly among 4 plates; distribute salsa evenly over rice. Top with cooked shrimp.

Nutrition facts
(per serving)

Calories: 461

Total fat: 10 grams

Saturated fat: 2 grams

Sodium: 199 mg

Carbohydrate: 58 grams

Fiber: 11 grams

Protein: 35 grams$

Spaghetti with Meatballs

Prep time: 15 minutes / Cook time: 30 minutes / Serves: 6 / Serving size: ⅙ mixture (2 ounces of pasta, 4 meatballs, and ½ cup sauce)

What you'll need

Sauce:

1 green bell pepper, chopped

1 onion, chopped

4 cloves garlic, chopped

1 (28 ounce) can no-salt-added whole tomatoes

½ cup low-sodium chicken stock

2 tablespoons Italian seasoning

1 (6 ounce) can no-salt-added tomato paste

1 tablespoon fresh basil, chopped fine

Meatballs:

1 pound lean ground meat

½ cup whole wheat bread crumbs

1 teaspoon dried basil

1 teaspoon Italian seasoning

2 tablespoons tomato sauce

1 egg

Pasta:

1 (12 ounce) package whole wheat spaghetti, cooked according to package directions

Parmesan cheese

What to do

1. Coat skillet with cooking spray. Over medium-high heat, sauté bell pepper and onion for 5 minutes.

2. Add garlic and sauté another minute. Stir in tomatoes, chicken broth, and Italian seasoning. Remove from heat.

3. Place mixture in blender and blend until desired level of chunkiness is achieved. Return to medium-low heat. Stir in tomato paste. Cook for 10 minutes, stirring occasionally. Add basil near end of cooking.

4. For meatballs, combine all meatball ingredients. Roll into 24 balls. Place on foil-lined cookie sheet and bake for 10 minutes or until no longer pink. Add to sauce and pour over hot spaghetti. Top with Parmesan cheese, if desired.

Nutrition Facts (per serving)

Calories: 460 / Total fat: 14 grams / Saturated fat: 5 grams / Sodium: 160 mg
Carbohydrate: 64 grams / Fiber: 10 grams / Protein: 24 grams / Cost: $$ / *

Spicy Stir-Fry Steak Fajitas

Prep time: 40 minutes / Cook time: 10 minutes / Makes: 6 servings / Serving size: 1 fajita

What you'll need

Marinade:

1 teaspoon grated lime zest

¼ cup fresh lime juice

1 tablespoon balsamic vinegar

2 cloves garlic, minced

⅛ teaspoon salt

½ teaspoon ground black pepper

¼ teaspoon ground cumin

Fajita filling:

1 pound top sirloin, trimmed of fat

1 tablespoon canola oil

1 medium red bell pepper, sliced thin

1 medium green bell pepper, sliced thin

1 jalapeño pepper, chopped

1 large onion, thinly sliced

6 whole wheat flour tortillas

Dash hot sauce

1 cup plain nonfat yogurt or Greek yogurt

What to do

1. In small bowl, combine all marinade ingredients. Thinly slice meat across grain and place in bowl. Cover and refrigerate for about 30 minutes.

2. Warm nonstick skillet over medium-high heat. Add oil, peppers, and onion. Stir-fry about 4 minutes. Increase heat to high and add meat to skillet. Stir-fry for about 5 minutes.

3. To serve, divide meat mixture evenly among 6 tortillas. Add hot sauce and yogurt to taste.

4. Roll tortillas; eat out of hand.

Nutrition facts
(per serving)

Calories: 324

Total fat: 10 grams

Saturated fat: 2 grams

Sodium: 259 mg

Carbohydrate: 36 grams

Fiber: 4 grams

Protein: 24 grams

Cost: $$$

Stuffed Bell Peppers

Prep time: 15 minutes / Cook time: 40 minutes / Makes: 4 servings / Serving size: ½ stuffed pepper

What you'll need

2 large green bell peppers
8 ounces ground sirloin
½ cup onions, chopped
3 cloves garlic, minced
1 cup cooked brown rice
1 (15 ounce) can no-salt-added diced tomatoes

2 tablespoons no-salt-added tomato paste
1 tablespoon Worcestershire sauce
½ teaspoon dried basil
½ teaspoon onion powder
½ teaspoon garlic powder

¼ teaspoon salt
¼ teaspoon ground black pepper
½ cup finely shredded reduced-fat cheddar cheese

What to do

1. Bring 16 cups of water in large saucepan to boil. Cut peppers lengthwise in half. Remove and discard stems, seeds, and membranes.

2. Place peppers in boiling water for 3 minutes. Remove peppers and put on paper towels to drain.

3. Preheat oven to 375 degrees. Lightly coat large skillet with cooking spray, warm to medium heat. Add beef, onions, and garlic. Cook over medium heat until beef is no longer pink, stirring occasionally. Drain and return to pan.

4. Stir in rice, tomatoes, tomato paste, Worcestershire sauce, basil, onion powder, garlic powder, salt, and pepper. Cover and simmer 10 minutes. Place pepper halves in an 8x8-inch baking dish. Spoon meat mixture into pepper shells. Sprinkle cheese on top. Bake 10 minutes.

Nutrition facts
per serving)

Calories: 264
Total fat: 8 grams
Saturated fat: 3 grams
Sodium: 344 mg
Carbohydrate: 25 grams
Fiber: 4 grams
Protein: 23 grams
Cost: $
*

Sweet and Sour Chicken

Prep time: 15 minutes / Cook time: 10 minutes / Makes: 4 servings / Serving size: ¼ mixture

What you'll need

2 tablespoons olive oil

1 pound boneless skinless chicken breasts, cut into large cubes

2 zucchini, sliced thin

1 red bell pepper, sliced thin

3 carrots, sliced thin

3 cloves garlic, chopped

1 tablespoon cornstarch

2 tablespoons light soy sauce

1 cup pineapple chunks, juice reserved

1 tablespoon white vinegar

1 tablespoon dark brown sugar

½ teaspoon ground ginger

⅛ teaspoon salt

¼ teaspoon ground black pepper

1 teaspoon sesame seeds

Brown rice, cooked

What to do

1. Warm large skillet to medium-high heat. Add oil and chicken and cook until no longer pink, about 5 minutes. Add zucchini, bell pepper, carrots, and garlic, cooking for an additional 5 minutes.

2. In small bowl, combine cornstarch, soy sauce, reserved pineapple juice, vinegar, brown sugar, ginger, salt, and pepper. Pour mixture into skillet; bring to boil.

3. Turn heat to medium-low and let simmer for 5 minutes. Stir in pineapple chunks and sesame seeds and heat thoroughly.

4. Serve over brown rice, if desired.

Nutrition facts (per serving)

Calories: 194 / Total fat: 10 grams / Saturated fat: 1 gram / Sodium: 409 mg
Carbohydrate: 23 grams / Fiber: 4 grams / Protein: 29 grams / Cost: $$ / *

Tomato and Eggplant Pasta

Prep time: 10 minutes / Cook time: 20 minutes / Makes: 8 servings / Serving size: 1¼ cups

What you'll need

1 tablespoon olive oil

1 medium-sized eggplant, cubed

1 red bell pepper, chopped

1 large yellow onion, chopped

4 cloves garlic, chopped

1 (30 ounce) can crushed tomatoes

⅛ teaspoon crushed red pepper flakes

1 teaspoon hot and spicy salt-free seasoning

½ teaspoon dried basil

½ teaspoon dried oregano

¼ teaspoon dried thyme

1 (16 ounce) box whole wheat penne pasta, cooked according to package directions

1 cup shredded Parmesan cheese

What to do

1. Warm oil in large, nonstick skillet over medium-high heat. Add eggplant, pepper, and onion; sauté for 7 minutes or until onion is softened. Stir in garlic and cook an additional 2 minutes. Add crushed tomatoes and seasonings; reduce heat to medium-low and simmer for 8 minutes.

2. Toss eggplant mixture with pasta in large bowl; sprinkle with cheese and stir well.

3. Serve warm.

Nutrition facts
(per serving)

Calories: 332

Total fat: 7 grams

Saturated fat: 3 grams

Sodium: 334 mg

Carbohydrate: 59 grams

Fiber: 11 grams

Protein: 12 grams

Cost: $$

Snack Recipes

Ambrosia

Prep time: 10 minutes / Chill time: 1 hour / Makes: 8 servings / Serving size: ⅛ mixture

What you'll need

½ cup slivered almonds

¼ cup flaked coconut

1 large pineapple, chopped

5 oranges, chopped

2 red apples, chopped

2 bananas, chopped

1 cup vanilla low-fat yogurt

2 cups fat-free whipped
topping

- -

What to do

1. Preheat oven to 375 degrees.

2. Spread almonds and coconut over large cookie sheet and bake in preheated oven for 5 minutes. Cool completely.

3. Combine all remaining ingredients in large bowl. Stir in toasted nuts and coconut.

4. Chill for one hour.

- -

Nutrition facts (per serving)

Calories: 265 / Total fat: 9 grams / Saturated fat: 0.5 grams / Sodium: 74 mg
Carbohydrate: 46 grams / Fiber: 5 grams / Protein: 5 grams / Cost: $$

Asparagus Salad

Prep time: 20 minutes / Cook time: 15 minutes / Makes: 6 servings / Serving size: ⅙ salad

What you'll need

- 2 pounds asparagus (about 2 bunches), trimmed
- 1 pint cherry tomatoes
- 1 tablespoon extra-virgin olive oil
- ½ teaspoon salt
- Freshly ground pepper, to taste
- 1 tablespoon fresh lemon juice
- 1 tablespoon fresh orange juice
- 1 tablespoon honey
- ½ teaspoon Dijon mustard
- 2 bunches (4 cups) salad greens
- 2 tablespoons fresh dill, finely chopped, optional

What to do

1. Preheat oven to 450 degrees.
2. Place asparagus in large bowl. Add tomatoes and oil and toss to coat. Spread into heavy roasting pan or rimmed baking sheet, spooning tomatoes between and on top of asparagus. Sprinkle with salt and add generous grinding of pepper. Roast until asparagus is crisp-tender and tomatoes are warmed and slightly crinkled, about 15 minutes. Set aside until ready to serve.
3. Whisk lemon juice, orange juice, honey, and mustard in medium bowl. Reserve half of dressing in small bowl.
4. Add salad greens to dressing bowl; toss to coat. Spread salad on platter. Arrange roasted asparagus on salad greens and top with tomatoes. Drizzle reserved dressing over asparagus and tomatoes; sprinkle with dill, if desired.
5. Serve warm or at room temperature.

Nutrition facts
(per serving)

Calories: 64
Total fat: 3 grams
Saturated fat: 0.4 grams
Sodium: 211 mg
Carbohydrate: 10 grams
Fiber: 3 grams
Protein: 3 grams
Cost: $$$

Baked Chicken Spring Rolls

Prep time: 15 minutes / Cook time: 25 minutes / Makes: 8 servings / Serving size: ⅛ mixture

What you'll need

½ pound cooked chicken breast

1 cup cabbage, finely shredded

¼ cup carrots, finely shredded

2 green onions, thinly sliced

2 tablespoons fresh cilantro, chopped

½ teaspoon sesame oil

1 tablespoon oyster sauce

2 teaspoons fresh ginger root, grated

1½ teaspoons garlic, minced

1 teaspoon chili sauce

1 tablespoon cornstarch

1 tablespoon water

12 (7 inch square) spring roll wrappers

4 teaspoons canola oil

What to do

1. Preheat oven to 425 degrees.

2. Place chicken in medium skillet; cook over medium-high heat until no longer pink. Remove from heat and drain, then chop fine.

3. In medium bowl mix chicken, cabbage, carrots, green onions, cilantro, sesame oil, oyster sauce, ginger, garlic, and chili sauce.

4. Mix cornstarch and water in small bowl.

5. Place 1 tablespoon of chicken mixture in center of spring roll wrappers. Roll wrappers around mixture, folding edges inward to close. Moisten fingers with cornstarch and water mixture and brush wrapper seams to seal.

6. Arrange spring rolls in single layer on medium baking sheet. Brush with oil. Bake in preheated oven 20 minutes, until hot and lightly browned. For crispier spring rolls, turn after 10 minutes.

Nutrition facts (per serving)

Calories: 184 / Total fat: 3 grams / Saturated fat: 0.4 grams / Sodium: 432 mg
Carbohydrate: 31 grams / Fiber: 1.5 grams / Protein: 10 grams / Cost: $$

Basil and Tomato Bruschetta

Prep time: 8 minutes / Cook time: 10 minutes / Makes: 36 slices / Serving size: 1 slice

What you'll need

2 tablespoons olive oil

1 pound plum tomatoes, seeded and chopped

4 ounces low-fat feta cheese

4 ounces low-fat Parmesan cheese, shredded

½ cup red onions, chopped

2 teaspoons dried basil

3 tablespoons fresh parsley, chopped

1 tablespoon black olives, chopped

Salt and pepper to taste, if desired

36 small slices French bread (about 2 loaves)

What to do

1. Preheat oven to 400 degrees.

2. Mix all ingredients except bread in medium bowl. Season mixture with salt and pepper, if desired.

3. Place bread on cookie sheet. Toast for about 3 minutes on each side. Remove from oven and top with tomato mixture.

4. Return to oven and bake an additional 3 minutes or until cheese is melted.

Nutrition facts
(per serving)

Calories: 54

Total fat: 2.3 grams

Saturated fat: 0.9 gram

Sodium: 267 mg

Carbohydrate: 19 grams

Fiber: 1 gram

Protein: 2 grams

Cost: $$

Black-Eyed Pea Dip

Prep time: 30 minutes / Chill time: 30 minutes / Makes: 10 servings / Serving size: 1 cup

What you'll need

3 cups cooked black-eyed peas
1 cup fresh corn kernels
1 cup red bell pepper, diced
½ cup red onion, minced
¼ cup fresh cilantro, chopped
1 tablespoon jalapeño, minced
 and seeded

¼ cup fresh lime juice
1 tablespoon lime zest
¼ cup red wine vinegar
1 tablespoon garlic, minced
1 tablespoon olive oil
2 teaspoons ground cumin
1 teaspoon chili powder

1 teaspoon onion powder
1 teaspoon garlic powder
½ teaspoon black pepper
Dash ground red pepper
1 cup tomato, diced
1 cup avocado, diced
Pita wedges

What to do

1. Combine first 6 ingredients in large bowl; stir well.

2. Combine juice, zest, vinegar, and next 8 ingredients (through red pepper) in small bowl. Stir with whisk.

3. Add juice mixture to bean mixture; toss well. Cover and chill 30 minutes. Gently stir in tomato and avocado. Serve warm or cold with pita wedges.

Nutrition facts
(per serving)

Calories: 129

Total fat: 4.2 grams

Saturated fat: 0.7 grams

Sodium: 11 mg

Carbohydrate: 20 grams

Fiber: 6 grams

Protein: 5 grams

Cost: $$

Broccoli Cheese Corn Bread

Prep time: 10 minutes / Cook time: 30 minutes / Makes: 12 servings (12 pieces) / Serving size: 1 piece

What you'll need

1½ cups self-rising cornmeal

2 eggs

2 egg whites

1 cup low-fat cottage cheese, low-sodium

1 onion, chopped

1 red bell pepper, chopped

¼ teaspoon black pepper

½ teaspoon onion powder

½ teaspoon garlic powder

½ cup light butter, melted

1 (10 ounce) package chopped frozen broccoli, thawed and drained

What to do

1. Preheat oven to 400 degrees. Lightly grease 11x17-inch baking pan.

2. In large mixing bowl, add cornmeal mix. In separate bowl, mix together eggs, cottage cheese, onion, red bell pepper, seasonings, and butter. Stir egg and cheese mixture into cornmeal. Mix in broccoli. Pour batter into prepared pan.

3. Bake in preheated oven for 30 minutes or until toothpick inserted in center of pan comes out clean.

Nutrition facts (per serving)

Calories: 102 / Total fat: 3 grams / Saturated fat: 1 gram / Sodium: 293 mg
Carbohydrate: 14 grams / Fiber: 2 grams / Protein: 6 grams / Cost: $$ / *

Lord, please bless this food as we thank You for giving it to us. We ask You to bless those who hunger and thirst. In Jesus' name, amen.

Carrot Soufflé

Prep time: 10 minutes / Cook time: 30 minutes / Makes: 8 servings / Serving size: ½ cup

What you'll need

3 cups carrots, sliced

1 tablespoon light butter

2 eggs

4 egg whites

½ cup sugar

½ cup spoonable sugar
    substitute

⅓ cup skim milk

½ teaspoon salt

1 teaspoon ground cinnamon

½ teaspoon ground nutmeg

1 teaspoon vanilla

What to do

1. Preheat oven to 350 degrees. Coat 9x13-inch glass baking dish with cooking spray; set aside.

2. Place carrots in saucepan, with enough water to cover them. Bring to boil and let cook for about 20 minutes. Drain and cool carrots. Puree carrots to smooth consistency in food processor or blender.

3. In medium bowl, mix carrots, butter, and remaining ingredients.

4. Spread mixture into prepared casserole dish.

5. Bake for 30 minutes.

Nutrition facts
(per serving)

Calories: 147

Total fat: 2 grams

Saturated fat: 0.6 grams

Sodium: 225 mg

Carbohydrate: 30 grams

Fiber: 1 gram

Protein: 4 grams

Cost: $

*

Cheesy Spinach Cakes

Prep time: 15 minutes / Cook time: 20 minutes / Makes: 4 servings / Serving size: 2 spinach cakes

What you'll need

1 medium yellow onion, diced

10 ounces frozen chopped spinach, thawed and drained*

½ cup part-skim ricotta cheese, or low-fat cottage cheese

2 large eggs, beaten

1 clove garlic, minced

¼ teaspoon salt

½ cup finely shredded Parmesan cheese, plus more for garnish

¼ teaspoon freshly ground pepper

*After spinach is thawed, place in paper towel and squeeze out as much liquid as you can over sink. This will prevent cakes from being too watery.

What to do

1. Preheat oven to 400 degrees.

2. Coat medium skillet with cooking spray. Over medium heat, sauté diced onion until tender and browned.

3. In medium bowl, add well-drained spinach, onion, ricotta (or cottage) cheese, Parmesan cheese, eggs, garlic, salt, and pepper; stir to combine.

4. Coat 8 cups of muffin pan with cooking spray. Divide spinach mixture among 8 cups. (They will be very full.)

5. Bake spinach cakes until set, about 20 minutes. Let stand in pan for 5 minutes. Loosen edges with knife and turn out onto clean cutting board or large plate. Serve warm, sprinkled with more Parmesan, if desired.

Nutrition facts (per serving)

Calories: 118 / Total fat: 5 grams / Saturated fat: 3 grams / Sodium: 390 mg
Carbohydrate: 7 grams / Fiber: 3 grams / Protein: 12 grams / Cost: $

Confetti Coleslaw

Prep time: 15 minutes / Chill time: 2 hours / Makes: 10 servings / Serving size: ½ cup

What you'll need

¼ cup honey

¼ cup extra-virgin olive oil

¼ cup apple cider vinegar

1 tablespoon poppy seeds

¼ teaspoon salt

1 teaspoon ground black pepper

3 cups green cabbage, shredded

1 cup carrots, shredded

1 cup purple cabbage, shredded

½ cup red onion, sliced fine

What to do

1. In large bowl, whisk honey, olive oil, vinegar, poppy seeds, salt, and pepper.

2. Add remaining ingredients.

3. Toss to coat evenly. Cover and refrigerate at least two hours before serving.

Nutrition facts
(per serving)

Calories: 92

Total fat: 6 grams

Saturated fat: 0.8 grams

Sodium: 69 mg

Carbohydrate: 7 grams

Fiber: 1.2 grams

Protein: 0.7 grams

Cost: $

Corn Pudding

Prep time: 10 minutes / Cook time: 50 minutes / Makes: 8 servings / Serving size: ½ cup

What you'll need

1 (15 ounce) can no-salt-added, whole kernel corn, drained

1 (15 ounce) can cream corn

1 cup fat-free skim milk

1 egg, beaten

2 egg whites, beaten

¼ cup light butter, melted

¼ teaspoon black pepper

¼ teaspoon onion powder

¼ teaspoon garlic powder

½ cup cornmeal

What to do

1. Preheat oven to 375 degrees.

2. Combine corns, milk, egg, egg whites, butter, and seasonings in large bowl; add cornmeal. Stir until moist.

3. Pour corn mixture into 2-quart casserole dish coated with cooking spray. Bake for 50 minutes or until casserole is golden brown.

Nutrition facts (per serving)

Calories: 170 / Total fat: 5 grams / Saturated fat: 2.7 grams / Sodium: 139 mg
Carbohydrate: 22 grams / Fiber: 2 grams / Protein: 5 grams / Cost: $

Giving God, help us remember that we are blessed so that we may feed others. In Your holy name we pray, amen.

Eggplant Dip with Toasted Cumin Pita Wedges

Prep time: 15 minutes / Cook time: 50 minutes / Makes: 6 servings / Serving size: about ⅓ cup dip and 5 pita wedges

What you'll need

Dip:
1 large eggplant
1 tablespoon extra-virgin olive oil
1 cup mushrooms, sliced thin
1 green bell pepper, seeded and diced
1 small yellow onion, diced
3 cloves garlic, minced
Juice from 1 lemon
Dash salt

Freshly ground black pepper to taste (about ¼ teaspoon)
¼ cup pine nuts
5 jumbo black olives, sliced thin
2 tablespoons flat leaf parsley, chopped

Pita wedges:
4 (4 inch) whole wheat pitas, split in half and cut into 4 wedges
1 tablespoon extra-virgin olive oil
2 teaspoons cumin
1 teaspoon onion powder
1 teaspoon garlic powder
2 teaspoons paprika
Dash salt

What to do

1. For dip: Preheat oven to 450 degrees. Place eggplant on cookie sheet lined with foil and coated with cooking spray. Prick skin of eggplant several times with fork. Bake eggplant for 40 minutes. Remove from oven and set aside to cool.

2. In nonstick skillet warmed to medium-high heat, add olive oil. Stir in mushrooms, green bell pepper, onion, and garlic. Sauté for about 5 minutes; set aside.

3. Slice eggplant in half lengthwise and scoop out flesh, discarding skin. Place eggplant flesh in food processor, then add sautéed vegetables, lemon juice, salt, and pepper. Process until smooth. Put mixture into serving bowl.

4. Place pine nuts on small cookie sheet and bake until golden, about 4 minutes.

5. Drop pine nuts and sliced black olives over eggplant dip. Sprinkle with parsley.

6. For pita chips: Preheat oven to 400 degrees. Place pita wedges on cookie sheet and brush with olive oil.

7. In small bowl, stir cumin, onion powder, garlic powder, paprika, and salt together.

8. Sprinkle seasoning mixture over pita wedges. Bake for 6 minutes.

Nutrition facts (per serving)

Calories: 173 / Total fat: 10 grams / Saturated fat: 1 gram / Sodium: 200 mg
Carbohydrate: 21 grams / Fiber: 5 grams / Protein: 4 grams / Cost: $$

Frozen Fruit Salad

Prep time: 18 minutes / Freeze time: 3 hours / Makes: 12 servings (12 squares) / Serving size: 1 square

What you'll need

8 ounces reduced-fat cream cheese, softened

½ cup spoonable sugar substitute

3 bananas, sliced

2 cups canned crushed pineapple, drained

2 cups frozen unsweetened strawberries, partially thawed and sliced

1 cup frozen cherries, partially thawed and sliced

2 ounces walnuts, chopped

2 cups light whipped topping, thawed

What to do

1. Coat 9x13-inch pan with cooking spray; set aside.

2. In large bowl, stir cream cheese and spoonable sugar substitute together. Add remaining ingredients and stir well.

3. Pour mixture into prepared pan.

4. Freeze for at least 3 hours.

5. Cut into 12 squares.

Nutrition facts
(per serving)

Calories: 189

Total fat: 8 grams

Saturated fat: 3 grams

Sodium: 105 mg

Carbohydrate: 29 grams

Fiber: 2 grams

Protein: 4 grams

Cost: $$

Fruit Salad with Lemon Sauce and Walnuts

Prep time: 10 minutes / Chill time: 1 hour / Makes: 6 servings / Serving size: ½ cup

What you'll need

½ cup fat-free sour cream

3 tablespoons powdered sugar

1 teaspoon grated lemon zest

1 teaspoon freshly squeezed lemon juice

1 teaspoon vanilla

1 cup green grapes

1 cup red grapes

1 cup strawberries, halved

1 ounce (14 halves) walnuts, crushed

What to do

1. In small bowl, stir sour cream, powdered sugar, lemon zest, juice, and vanilla; blend until smooth.

2. In large bowl, mix remaining ingredients.

3. Pour sour cream mixture over fruit.

4. Chill at least 1 hour.

Nutrition facts (per serving)

Calories: 107 / Total fat: 3 grams / Saturated fat: 3 grams / Sodium: 15 mg
Carbohydrate: 19 grams / Fiber: 1 gram / Protein: 3 grams / Cost: $

Dear Jesus, we thank You for this food to nourish our bodies.

May we be a blessing to others, in Your name we pray. Amen.

Granola with Cherries and Raisins

Prep time: 5 minutes / Cook time: 1 hour / Makes: 24 servings / Serving size: about ⅓ cup

What you'll need

5 cups oats

1 cup almonds

1 cup walnuts

½ cup shredded unsweetened
   coconut

¼ cup dark brown sugar

½ cup pure maple syrup

¼ cup canola oil

½ teaspoon salt

1 teaspoon ground cinnamon

½ cup dried cherries

½ cup raisins

What to do

1. Preheat oven to 300 degrees.
2. In large bowl, combine oats, almonds, walnuts, coconut, and brown sugar.
3. In separate bowl, combine maple syrup, oil, salt, and cinnamon.
4. Pour syrup mixture into oat mixture and blend well. Pour onto 3 cookie sheets that have been coated with cooking spray. Cook for 1 hour, stirring every 15 minutes.
5. Remove from oven and stir in dried fruit.

Serving suggestions: This granola is delicious in a bowl with milk, sprinkled on top of yogurt or ice cream, or all by itself!

Nutrition facts
(per serving)

Calories: 192

Total fat: 1 gram

Saturated fat: 1.2 grams

Sodium: 51 mg

Carbohydrate: 25 grams

Fiber: 3 grams

Protein: 5 grams

Cost: $$

Green Beans with Cherry Tomatoes

Prep time: 15 minutes / Cook time: 12 minutes / Makes: 6 servings / Serving size: 1 cup

What you'll need

2 shallots, sliced thin

2 tablespoons white wine
vinegar

1 pound trimmed fresh
green beans

3 cloves garlic, minced

3 tablespoons extra-virgin
olive oil

3 tablespoons fresh basil,
chopped

Dash sea salt

¼ teaspoon ground black
pepper

1 tablespoon red wine vinegar

1 cup cherry tomatoes, halved

What to do

1. In medium mixing bowl, stir together shallots and vinegar; set aside.

2. Bring large pot of water to boil; add green beans and cook for about 8 minutes. Drain.

3. Place beans in large bowl; add remaining ingredients along with reserved shallots and vinegar
   and toss well.

4. Serve warm or cold.

Nutrition facts (per serving)

Calories: 96 / Total fat: 7 grams / Saturated fat: 1 gram / Sodium: 24 mg
Carbohydrate: 8 grams / Fiber: 3 grams / Protein: 2 grams / Cost: $$

Guacamole Dip

Prep time: 10 minutes / Makes: 6 servings / Serving size: ¼ cup

What you'll need

3 avocadoes, peeled and diced

1 cup tomatoes, seeded and diced

½ cup white onion, finely minced

¼ cup cilantro, chopped

2 limes, juiced

½ teaspoon sea salt

What to do

1. In medium bowl, combine all ingredients. Stir well.
2. Cover with plastic wrap and chill until ready to serve.

Serving suggestions: This dip is great on burgers, quesadillas, tacos, or with tortilla chips.

Nutrition facts
(per serving)

Calories: 197

Total fat: 15 grams

Saturated fat: 3 grams

Sodium: 200 mg

Carbohydrate: 16 grams

Fiber: 9 grams

Protein: 2 grams

Cost: $$

Honey Glazed Fruit Salad

Prep time: 15 minutes / Makes: 10 servings / Serving size: ½ cup

What you'll need

11 ounces mandarin oranges

2 cups strawberries. sliced

1 cup banana, sliced

1 apple, sliced

1 ounce walnuts, chopped

¼ cup raisins

1 avocado, chopped

Juice and zest from 1 lemon

½ cup orange juice

⅓ cup honey

1 teaspoon poppy seeds

What to do

1. In large bowl, toss all fruit, nuts, raisins, and avocado.

2. In small bowl, mix lemon juice and zest, orange juice, honey, and poppy seeds.

3. Pour over fruit. Stir well.

Nutrition facts
(per serving)

Calories: 149

Total fat: 5 grams

Saturated fat: 1 gram

Sodium: 4 mg

Fiber: 4 grams

Protein: 2 grams

Cost: $$

Hummus

Prep time: 10 minutes / Makes: 8 servings / Serving size: ¼ cup

What you'll need

1 can chickpeas, rinsed and drained

2 tablespoons fresh lemon juice

3 tablespoons tahini paste

3 tablespoons water

3 cloves garlic, minced

2 tablespoons olive oil

1 teaspoon ground cumin

½ teaspoon salt

½ teaspoon pepper

Pita chips

What to do

1. Combine all ingredients in blender or food processor. Run until smooth.

2. Serve with baked pita chips.

Nutrition facts (per serving)

Calories: 105 / Total fat: 4 grams / Saturated fat: 1 gram / Sodium: 163 mg
Carbohydrate: 14 grams / Fiber: 3 grams / Protein: 3 grams / Cost: $

*Store hummus in refrigerator for up to 10 days.

Gracious Lord, I thank You for the food I am about to receive,

the sources from which it came, and the hands that prepared it.

May this food provide proper nourishment to my body.

In Your name I pray, amen.

Italian Spinach

Prep time: 5 minutes / Cook time: 5 minutes / Makes: 4 servings / Serving size: ¼ mixture

What you'll need

1 (10 ounce) box frozen chopped spinach

2 tablespoons extra-virgin olive oil

2 cloves garlic, minced

Dash salt

Freshly ground black pepper, to taste

2 eggs

2 tablespoons grated reduced-fat Parmesan cheese

What to do

1. Thaw spinach and squeeze out water with paper towels; set aside.
2. In skillet set over medium heat, add olive oil and garlic; cook until garlic is fragrant and golden brown.
3. Add spinach, salt, and pepper; sauté for about 3 minutes.
4. Break in eggs; sauté and stir until eggs are cooked and thoroughly mixed into spinach. Drain and place into serving bowl.
5. Sprinkle Parmesan cheese on top.
6. Serve warm.

Nutrition facts (per serving)

Calories: 121 / Total fat: 10 grams / Saturated fat: 2 grams / Sodium: 146 mg
Carbohydrate: 3 grams / Cholesterol: 107 grams / Fiber: 2 grams / Protein: 6 grams
Cost: $

Jalapeño Corn Bread Muffins

Prep time: 10 minutes / Cook time: 15 minutes / Makes: 12 servings / Serving size: 1 muffin

What you'll need

1½ cups cornmeal

1 cup fat-free sour cream

¼ cup jalapeño peppers, chopped and seeded

2 tablespoons canola oil

2 tablespoons dark molasses

¾ teaspoon baking powder

¾ teaspoon baking soda

½ teaspoon salt

1 egg

2 large egg whites, lightly beaten

1 (14¾ ounce) can cream-style corn

What to do

1. Preheat oven to 400 degrees.

2. Coat 12-muffin tin with cooking spray.

3. Combine all ingredients in large bowl.

4. Pour mixture evenly into muffin tins.

5. Bake for 25 minutes or until toothpick inserted in center comes out clean.

6. Cool in pan for 10 minutes on wire rack.

7. Remove from pan.

Nutrition facts
(per serving)

Calories: 136

Total fat: 4 grams

Saturated fat: 1 gram

Sodium: 395 mg

Carbohydrate: 24 grams

Fiber: 2 grams

Protein: 4 grams

Cost: $

*

Kale Chips

Prep time: 15 minutes / Cook time: 10 minutes / Makes: 6 servings / Serving size: about ½ cup

What you'll need

1 bunch of kale   1 tablespoon of olive oil

Variations (choose one):

½ teaspoon sea salt
2 tablespoons Parmesan
   cheese

½ teaspoon cinnamon,
   ½ teaspoon sugar, ½
   teaspoon Splenda (for
   kettle chips)

½ teaspoon sea salt and 1
   teaspoon red pepper flakes
1 tablespoon balsamic vinegar
   and ½ teaspoon sea salt
   (for salt and vinegar chips)

- -

What to do

1. Preheat oven to 350 degrees.

2. Wash and thoroughly dry kale. Tear into bite-sized pieces and place in gallon-size zip-top bag.

3. Pour 1 tablespoon of olive oil into bag and shake until kale is thoroughly coated.

4. Add favorite seasonings from list above and shake until evenly distributed.

5. Spread chips on foil-lined cookie sheet and bake for 8 to 10 minutes. Edges should be brown, but not burned.

Nutrition facts
(per serving, based on sea salt variation)

Calories: 57

Total fat: 3 grams

Saturated fat: 0 grams

Sodium: 226 mg

Carbohydrate: 8 grams

Fiber: 2 grams

Protein: 1 gram

Cost: $

Lemon Green Beans

Prep time: 10 minutes / Cook time: 10 minutes / Makes: 4 servings / Serving size: ½ cup

What you'll need

1 tablespoon light unsalted butter

½ tablespoon extra-virgin olive oil

1 garlic clove, halved

2 cups green beans, washed and trimmed

1 teaspoon lemon zest

½ teaspoon oregano

½ teaspoon dried parsley

¼ teaspoon salt

½ teaspoon black pepper

What to do

1. Warm butter, olive oil, and garlic together over very low heat for about 2 minutes. Remove from heat and allow garlic to sit in butter mixture for about five minutes.

2. Bring large pot of water to boil; add washed and trimmed green beans. Boil until slightly tender, about 5 minutes.

3. Drain beans and quickly rinse under cold water for a few seconds. (This helps to stop the cooking process and keeps them nice and green!)

4. Remove garlic from butter mixture and toss green beans in garlic-infused butter.

5. Add lemon zest, oregano, parsley, salt, and pepper. Toss to coat.

Nutrition facts (per serving)

Calories: 50 / Total fat: 1 gram / Saturated fat: 0 gram / Sodium: 152 mg
Carbohydrate: 4 grams / Fiber: 2 grams / Protein: 1 gram / Cost: $

Mediterranean Roasted Tomatoes and Broccoli

Prep time: 10 minutes / Cook time: 20 minutes / Makes: 4 servings / Serving size: about 1 cup

What you'll need

12 ounces broccoli crowns, trimmed and cut into bite-sized florets (about 4 cups)

1 cup grape tomatoes

1 tablespoon extra-virgin olive oil

2 cloves garlic, minced

¼ teaspoon salt

½ teaspoon freshly grated lemon zest

1 tablespoon lemon juice (about half a lemon)

10 pitted black olives

1 teaspoon dried oregano (or Italian herb blend)

What to do

1. Preheat oven to 450 degrees.

2. Toss broccoli, tomatoes, oil, garlic, and salt in large bowl until evenly coated. Spread in even layer on baking sheet. Bake 10 to 13 minutes, until broccoli begins to brown.

3. Meanwhile, combine lemon zest and juice, olives, and oregano in large bowl. Add roasted vegetables; stir to combine. Serve warm.

Nutrition facts (per serving)

Calories: 77 / Total fat: 5 grams / Saturated fat: 1 gram / Sodium: 263 mg
Carbohydrate: 8 grams / Fiber: 1 gram / Protein: 3 grams / Cost: $$

Oven-Fried Okra

Prep time: 15 minutes / Cook time: 15 minutes / Makes: 6 servings / Serving size: ½ cup

What you'll need

1 pound fresh okra pods, trimmed and cut into ¾-inch slices (about 3 cups)

2 slices of whole wheat bread, toasted

2 egg whites

½ cup cornmeal

1 teaspoon onion powder

1 teaspoon garlic powder

¼ teaspoon ground red pepper

⅛ teaspoon salt

¼ teaspoon pepper

What to do

1. Preheat oven to 450 degrees.

2. In large pot, bring okra to boil for 5 minutes. Drain and pat dry.

3. While okra is boiling, place toasted bread in food processor. Run until bread crumbs form; set aside.

4. In medium bowl, whisk egg whites. Add okra to bowl and stir until coated with egg mixture.

5. Fill one-gallon zip-top bag with cornmeal, homemade bread crumbs, and spices. Using slotted spoon, remove okra from egg mixture and add to bag. Shake until okra is evenly coated.

6. Line baking sheet with foil and coat with cooking spray. Spread okra in single layer.

7. Bake 12 to 15 minutes, until crisp and golden brown.

Nutrition facts
(per serving)

Calories: 135

Total fat: 4 grams

Saturated fat: 0 grams

Sodium: 118 mg

Carbohydrate: 21 grams

Fiber: 4 grams

Protein: 6 grams

Cost: $$

Peanut Butter Bars

Prep time: 5 minutes / Chill time: 30 minutes / Makes: 24 bars / Serving size: 1 bar

What you'll need

4 ounces dark chocolate chips

3 cups oats

2 cups reduced-fat peanut butter

1 cup honey

What to do

1. Mix all ingredients thoroughly in large bowl.

2. Press to bottom of 9x13-inch baking pan coated with cooking spray.

3. Chill for at least 30 minutes.

4. Cut into 24 bars.

5. Store leftover bars in refrigerator.

Nutrition facts
(per serving)

Calories: 203

Total fat: 8.2 grams

Saturated fat: 2 grams

Sodium: 102 mg

Carbohydrate: 25 grams

Fiber: 2 grams

Protein: 6 grams

Cost: $$

Pumpkin Raisin Bars

Prep time: 15 minutes / Cook time: 30 minutes / Makes: 12 bars / Serving size: 1 bar

What you'll need

2 eggs

⅓ cup 100% bran cereal

¼ cup flour

2 teaspoons baking powder

1 teaspoon pumpkin pie spice

¼ cup (½ stick) light butter
   or margarine, softened

½ cup firmly packed brown
   sugar substitute

½ cup canned pumpkin

½ cup raisins

Powdered sugar (optional)

What to do

1. Beat eggs in small bowl. Stir in bran; let stand 5 minutes.

2. Mix flour, baking powder, and pumpkin pie spice in another small bowl.

3. With electric mixer on medium speed, beat butter and sugar in large bowl until light and fluffy.

4. Beat in cereal mixture and pumpkin. Stir in flour mixture and raisins until well blended.
   Spread batter in greased and floured 9-inch square baking pan.

5. Bake at 350 degrees for 25 to 30 minutes or until toothpick inserted in center comes out clean.

6. Cool in pan on wire rack. Sprinkle with powdered sugar, if desired. Cut into squares.

Nutrition facts (per serving)

Calories: 87 / Total fat: 4 grams / Saturated fat: 2 grams / Sodium: 55 mg
Carbohydrate: 13 grams / Fiber: 2 grams / Protein: 2 grams / Cost: $

Heavenly Father, we thank You for this food and ask that You bless and

sanctify it for the nourishment of our bodies. In Jesus' name, amen.

Roasted Brussels Sprouts with Bacon

Prep time: 10 minutes / Cook time: 30 minutes / Makes: 10 servings / Serving size: 1 cup

What you'll need

4 thick slices bacon, cut into 1-inch pieces

1 large onion, diced

3 pounds fresh or frozen Brussels sprouts, trimmed

1 tablespoon extra-virgin olive oil

½ teaspoon salt

¼ teaspoon ground black pepper

What to do

1. Preheat oven to 350 degrees. Coat large cookie sheet with cooking spray; set aside.
2. Cook bacon in large skillet over medium heat; stir for about 5 minutes. Remove bacon from skillet and let drain on paper towel.
3. Place onion in same skillet and sauté for about 5 minutes over medium heat.
4. Place Brussels sprouts on prepared cookie sheet. Pour olive oil, salt, and pepper on top. Distribute evenly over Brussels sprouts.
5. Roast in oven for 20 minutes. Remove from oven, and add prepared bacon and onions.
6. Place back in oven for an additional 10 minutes.

Nutrition facts
(per serving)

Calories: 127

Total fat: 7 grams

Saturated fat: 2 grams

Sodium: 244 mg

Carbohydrate: 14 grams

Fiber: 5 grams

Protein: 6 grams

Cost: $$

Roasted Ginger Cauliflower with Turmeric

Prep time: 5 minutes / Cook time: 30 minutes / Makes: 4 servings / Serving size: ¼ mixture

What you'll need

1 large head cauliflower, cut into florets

1 large jalapeño, seeded and minced

2 tablespoons extra-virgin olive oil

1 tablespoon fresh ginger, grated

1 tablespoon yellow mustard seeds

1 teaspoon ground turmeric

Dash salt

What to do

1. Preheat oven to 400 degrees. Coat lined cookie sheet with cooking spray.

2. Place cauliflower in bowl.

3. Add remaining ingredients and stir until all cauliflower is coated with olive oil and spices. Place cauliflower mixture on cookie sheet.

4. Bake in preheated oven for 20 to 30 minutes, or until desired tenderness is reached.

Nutrition facts (per serving)

Calories: 116 / Total fat: 4 grams / Saturated fat: 1 gram / Sodium: 54 mg
Carbohydrate: 10 grams / Fiber: 5 grams / Protein: 5 grams / Cost: $

Roasted Vegetable Medley

Prep time: 15 minutes / Cook time: 40 minutes / Makes: 8 servings / Serving size: ⅛ mixture

What you'll need

2 large eggplants, cubed and peeled

4 small zucchini, cubed

4 small yellow squash, cubed

1 large red onion, diced

4 cloves garlic, chopped

¼ cup olive oil

Dash salt

½ teaspoon black pepper

¼ cup fresh basil, chopped

2 teaspoons salt-free herb seasoning

¼ cup fresh chives, chopped

Juice from 1 lemon

What to do

1. Preheat oven to 375 degrees.

2. Line large cookie sheet with foil. Coat with cooking spray.

3. Place all ingredients in large bowl and stir well.

4. Pour mixture onto cookie sheet and bake in preheated oven for 40 minutes.

Nutrition facts
(per serving)

Calories: 118

Total fat: 7 grams

Saturated fat: 1 gram

Sodium: 23 mg

Carbohydrate: 13 grams

Fiber: 6 grams

Protein: 3 grams

Cost: $

Roasted Veggie Tart

Prep time: 15 minutes / Cook time: 45 minutes / Makes: 16 square slices / Serving size: 1 square

What you'll need

Crust:

2 cups white whole wheat flour

½ teaspoon salt

Fresh cracked black pepper

½ teaspoon Italian seasoning

½ cup olive oil

5½ tablespoons very cold club soda

Parchment paper

Filling:

1 medium onion, sliced

1 medium tomato, sliced

2 medium zucchini, sliced

2 small eggplant, sliced

1 medium red bell pepper, sliced

2 garlic cloves, chopped

2 teaspoons olive oil

¼ teaspoon sea salt

Black pepper

½ cup Spinach Basil Spread (from page 203)

What to do

1. For crust: In medium bowl whisk together flour, salt, black pepper, and Italian seasoning; set aside. In separate small bowl, whisk oil and club soda until creamy, about 2 minutes.

2. Pour oil mixture over flour mixture and stir together with fork, until flour comes together like dough.

3. Divide dough into two equal parts and roll gently between two sheets of parchment paper, in single direction. Remove top parchment paper. Trim edges and prick crust with fork.

4. Bake crust on parchment paper at 400 degrees for 12 minutes.

5. For filling: Place sliced vegetables in gallon-sized zip-top bag. Add olive oil and seasonings and shake until well coated.

6. Place vegetables on foil-lined cookie sheet and roast at 400 degrees for 25 minutes.

7. To assemble tart, allow crust to cool. Spread ¼ cup Spinach Basil Spread on each tart. Arrange roasted vegetables on top of tart. Sprinkle with sea salt, black pepper, and cooking spray.

8. Bake tart in oven for 2 minutes or just until warm at 350 degrees.

Nutrition facts (per serving, not including Spinach Basil Spread)

Calories: 92 / Total fat: 1 gram / Saturated fat: 0 gram / Sodium: 314 mg
Carbohydrate: 19 grams / Fiber: 3 grams / Protein: 3 grams / Cost: $$

Roasted Red Pepper Bean Dip

Prep time: 10 minutes / Cook time: 5 minutes / Makes: 8 servings / Serving size: ¼ cup

What you'll need

1 teaspoon olive oil

1 cup chopped onions

3 cloves garlic, minced

2 tablespoons fresh basil, chopped

2 tablespoons white wine vinegar

1 (15 ounce) can navy beans, drained and rinsed

8 ounces bottled-roasted red bell peppers, drained and chopped

Pita chips

What to do

1. Warm oil in medium, nonstick skillet over medium heat. Add onions and garlic; sauté 5 minutes or until onions are tender.

2. Combine onion mixture, basil, vinegar, beans, and peppers in food processor. Process until smooth.

3. Cover with plastic wrap and chill until ready to serve. Serve with pita chips.

Nutrition facts (per serving)

Calories: 80 / Total fat: 1 gram / Saturated fat: 0 grams / Sodium: 310 mg
Carbohydrate: 14 grams / Fiber: 3 grams / Protein: 5 grams / Cost: $

Rosemary Potatoes

Prep time: 10 minutes / Cook time: 15 minutes / Makes: 6 servings / Serving size: ⅙ mixture

What you'll need

6 large red potatoes, scrubbed
 clean and sliced thin

3 tablespoons fresh rosemary,
 finely chopped

2 tablespoons extra-virgin
 olive oil

Salt and pepper to taste,
 if desired

What to do

1. Preheat oven to 375 degrees.
2. Coat large foil-lined cookie sheet with cooking spray.
3. Put all ingredients in bowl and toss to coat.
4. Place on cookie sheet.
5. Bake in preheated oven for 15 minutes or until desired crispness.

Nutrition facts
(per serving)

Calories: 205

Total fat: 5 grams

Saturated fat: 1 gram

Sodium: 13 mg

Carbohydrate: 40 grams

Fiber: 5 grams

Protein: 4 grams

Cost: $

Scalloped Potatoes

Prep time: 15 minutes / Cook time: 1 hour / Makes: 8 servings / Serving size: about ½ cup

What you'll need

3 tablespoons light butter

3 tablespoons flour

1½ cups skim milk

½ teaspoon salt

Dash cayenne pepper

1 teaspoon onion powder

1 teaspoon garlic powder

1½ cups 2% cheddar cheese, grated, divided

4 cups potatoes, thinly sliced

What to do

1. Preheat oven to 350 degrees.

2. In small saucepan, melt butter and blend in flour; stir for one minute.

3. Add milk, stirring with whisk. Blend in salt, pepper, onion powder, and garlic powder.

4. Cook sauce on low until smooth and boiling, stirring occasionally with whisk.

5. Reduce heat to medium low and stir in 1 cup cheese.

6. Place half sliced potatoes in lightly sprayed 1-quart casserole dish.

7. Pour half of cheese sauce over potatoes.

8. Repeat with second layer of potatoes and cheese sauce.

9. Sprinkle remaining cheese on top.

10. Bake uncovered for about 1 hour at 350 degrees.

Nutrition facts (per serving)

Calories: 176 / Total fat: 8 grams / Saturated fat: 5 grams / Sodium: 352 mg
Carbohydrate: 19 grams / Fiber: 2 grams / Protein: 9 grams / Cost: $

Smokey Greens

Prep time: 10 minutes / Cook time: 1 hour / Makes: 8 servings / Serving size: ½ cup

What you'll need

3 bunches turnip greens

3 bunches mustard greens

1 tablespoon extra-virgin olive oil

½ cup red onion, diced

4 cloves garlic, minced

1 cup water

1 large dried smoked pepper

2 tablespoons apple cider vinegar

Fresh ground black pepper and salt to taste, if desired

What to do

1. Wash and trim greens.

2. Warm oil in large stockpot over medium heat. Add onion and garlic and sauté for 3 minutes or until onion is soft.

3. Add remaining ingredients. Cover, reduce heat to medium low and simmer for 1 hour. Stir every 15 minutes and add more water, if necessary. Season to taste with salt and pepper if desired.

Nutrition facts
(per serving)

Calories: 58

Total fat: 3 grams

Saturated fat: 0 grams

Sodium: 67 mg

Carbohydrate: 6 grams

Fiber: 4 grams

Protein: 4 grams

Cost: $$

*

Spiced Popcorn

Prep time: 10 minutes / Makes: 4 servings / Serving size: 3 cups

What you'll need

12 cups air-popped popcorn

2 tablespoons light butter, melted

½ teaspoon salt

2 teaspoons chili powder

2 teaspoons brown sugar

1 teaspoon ground cumin

1 teaspoon garlic powder

¼ teaspoon ground cayenne pepper

What to do

1. Place popcorn in large bowl. Add melted butter and mix well.
2. In small bowl, mix together seasonings.
3. Sprinkle over popcorn and blend well with hands or tongs.

Nutrition facts
(per serving)

Calories: 142

Total fat: 5 grams

Saturated fat: 3 grams

Sodium: 309 mg

Carbohydrate: 22 grams

Fiber: 4 grams

Protein: 4 grams

Cost: $

Spinach and Cheese Stuffed Squash

Prep time: 15 minutes / Cook time: 23 minutes / Makes: 5 servings / Serving size: 2 squash halves

What you'll need

5 medium yellow squash

1 cup frozen chopped spinach, thawed

4 ounces light cream cheese, softened

1 teaspoon Italian seasoning

½ teaspoon onion powder

½ teaspoon garlic powder

¼ cup red bell peppers, chopped fine

¼ cup yellow onion, chopped fine

¼ cup seasoned bread crumbs

Dash salt

⅛ teaspoon ground black pepper

2 tablespoons low-fat Parmesan cheese, shredded

What to do

1. Slice squash lengthwise. Use small spoon to scoop seeds from squash.

2. Combine remaining ingredients except cheese in large bowl; blend well.

3. Fill squash with equal portions of this mixture.

4. Place in 9x13-inch glass baking pan coated with cooking spray. Top squash with grated Parmesan cheese.

5. Bake in preheated oven for 23 minutes or until squash is tender.

Nutrition facts (per serving)

Calories: 122 / Total fat: 5 grams / Saturated fat: 3 grams / Sodium: 289 mg
Carbohydrate: 15 grams / Fiber: 4 grams / Protein: 7 grams / Cost: $$

For the food we share, for the friends that have gathered,

for the many blessings of life—for these and all things we praise and

thank You, Lord. In Jesus' name, amen.

Spinach Artichoke Dip

Prep time: 15 minutes / Cook time: 35 minutes / Makes: 10 servings / Serving size: ¼ cup

What you'll need

1 tablespoon extra-virgin olive oil

½ cup onions, chopped

3 cloves garlic, chopped

2 teaspoons flour

3 ounces light cream cheese

¾ cup skim milk

Dash salt

½ teaspoon black pepper

Onion powder and garlic powder to taste, if desired

10 ounces frozen chopped spinach, thawed and squeezed dry

1 cup chopped jarred artichoke hearts

1 cup shredded low-fat mozzarella cheese

Baked chips

What to do

1. Preheat oven to 375 degrees.

2. Warm oil in medium saucepan over medium-high heat. Add onions and garlic, cook for about 3 minutes, stirring constantly until onions and garlic are tender. Add flour and stir for 30 seconds. Add cream cheese and milk, cooking until cream cheese is thoroughly melted and mixture is thickened. Season with salt, pepper, onion powder, and garlic powder.

3. Place spinach and artichoke hearts in large bowl, pouring milk mixture over vegetables. Stir well. Place in an 8-inch glass baking dish coated with cooking spray. Top with shredded mozzarella cheese.

4. Bake in preheated oven for 15 minutes or until heated through.

5. Serve with baked chips.

Nutrition facts (per serving, excluding baked chips)

Calories: 94 / Total fat: 5 grams / Saturated fat: 2 grams / Sodium: 151 mg
Carbohydrate: 7 grams / Fiber: 2 grams / Protein: 6 grams / Cost: $$ / *

Spinach Basil Spread

Prep time: 15 minutes / Cook time: 30 minutes / Makes: 2 cups / Serving size: 2 tablespoons

What you'll need

1 (15 ounce) can reduced-sodium chickpeas

¼ cup tahini

2 tablespoons olive oil

Juice of 1 lemon

1 teaspoon salt

½ teaspoon black pepper

½ cup water

1 garlic clove

½ cup fresh basil

1 cup fresh spinach

What to do

1. Drain and rinse chickpeas.

2. Put all ingredients into food processor and process until smooth. If mixture is too thick, add 1 tablespoon water.

Nutrition facts
(per serving)

Calories: 48

Total fat: 2 grams

Saturated fat: 0 gram

Sodium: 225 mg

Carbohydrate: 6 grams

Fiber: 1 gram

Protein: 1 gram

Cost: $

Spinach Casserole

Prep time: 10 minutes / Cook time: 40 minutes / Makes: 12 servings / Serving size: 1/12 casserole

What you'll need

16 ounces low-fat, low-sodium cottage cheese

3 eggs

3 egg whites

½ cup flour

¼ cup light sour cream

Dash salt

¼ teaspoon freshly ground black pepper

½ teaspoon onion powder

½ teaspoon garlic powder

2 (10 ounce) packages frozen chopped spinach, thawed and drained

2 cups 2% shredded cheddar cheese, divided

What to do

1. Preheat oven to 350 degrees.

2. Coat 9x13-inch glass baking dish with cooking spray; set aside.

3. Place cottage cheese, eggs, egg whites, flour, sour cream, and all seasonings in food processor. Process until smooth.

4. Mix spinach, cottage cheese mixture, and 1 cup shredded cheese in bowl, then spread into prepared baking dish.

5. Bake in preheated oven for 30 minutes. Top with remaining shredded cheese and bake an additional 10 minutes or until cheese is melted and golden brown.

Nutrition facts (per serving)

Calories: 119 / Total fat: 4 grams / Saturated fat: 2 grams / Sodium: 205 mg
Carbohydrate: 8 grams / Fiber: 2 grams / Protein: 14 grams / Cost: $$ / *

Spinach Diamond Puffs

Prep time: 15 minutes / Cook time: 18 minutes / Makes: 32 appetizers / Serving size: 1 appetizer

What you'll need

½ cup carrots, grated

½ cup yellow or white onion, finely chopped

10 ounces frozen chopped spinach, thawed and drained

½ cup light sour cream

¼ teaspoon ground nutmeg

Dash salt

4 ounces shredded part skim mozzarella cheese

1 package frozen puff pastry sheets, thawed

¼ cup egg substitute, lightly beaten

1 tablespoon water

What to do

1. Preheat oven to 425 degrees.
2. Cover 2 cookie sheets with parchment paper.
3. Heat large, nonstick skillet to medium high. Coat with cooking spray.
4. Add carrots and onion. Sauté until both are tender, about 3 minutes.
5. Place carrots and onion mixture in medium mixing bowl. Add spinach, sour cream, all seasonings, and cheese; stir well.
6. Lightly roll one pastry sheet into 12-inch square. Using pizza cutter, cut rolled pastry into 16 3-inch squares.
7. Place small amount (about 1 tablespoon) of mixture in center of each square then bring 2 opposite corners of each square up over filling, pinching together firmly and twisting. Place squares on cookie sheet.
8. In small bowl, mix egg substitute and water.
9. Brush egg wash over each appetizer.
10. Bake in preheated oven for about 18 minutes.

Nutrition facts
(per serving)

Calories: 48

Total fat: 3 grams

Saturated fat: 1 gram

Sodium: 54 mg

Carbohydrate: 5 grams

Fiber: 1 gram

Protein: 2 grams

Cost: $$

Strawberry Spinach Salad

Prep time: 20 minutes / Makes: 8 servings / Serving size: ⅛ salad mixture (about 1½ cups)

What you'll need

12 cups baby spinach, washed and dried

3 cups strawberries, washed, dried, and halved

1 cup mandarin oranges, packed in own juice, drained

1 small red onion, sliced thin

3 tablespoons canola oil

¼ cup white wine vinegar

¼ cup spoonable sugar substitute

1 teaspoon paprika

1 tablespoon sesame seeds

1 tablespoon poppy seeds

Salt and pepper to taste, if desired

What to do

1. In large bowl, combine spinach, strawberries, oranges, and red onion.

2. In medium bowl, whisk remaining ingredients.

3. Pour over spinach mixture. With tongs, toss well to coat.

4. Cover and chill until ready to serve.

Nutrition facts
(per serving)

Calories: 118

Total fat: 6 grams

Saturated fat: 1 gram

Sodium: 39 mg

Carbohydrate: 16 grams

Fiber: 3 grams

Protein: 2 grams

Cost: $$

Sweet Potato and Granny Smith Apple Casserole

Prep time: 10 minutes / Cook time: 60 minutes / Makes: 8 servings / Serving size: ⅛ of recipe (about ½ cup)

What you'll need

3 large sweet potatoes, peeled and quartered

½ cup pure maple syrup

1 teaspoon ground cinnamon

½ teaspoon ground nutmeg

2 large Granny Smith apples, peeled and cut into ¼-inch slices

¼ cup white whole wheat flour

¼ cup dark brown sugar, packed

¼ cup light butter, softened

¼ cup walnuts, chopped

What to do

1. Place sweet potatoes in large saucepan with enough water to cover. Bring to boil and cook for about 30 minutes. Drain, cool, and cut into small slices.

2. Preheat oven to 350 degrees. Coat 9x13-inch baking dish with cooking spray.

3. In small bowl, stir together maple syrup, cinnamon, and nutmeg.

4. Layer sweet potatoes, maple syrup mixture, and apples in baking dish.

5. In medium bowl, mix flour, brown sugar, butter, and walnuts.

6. Sprinkle over sweet potatoes and bake for 30 minutes.

Nutrition facts (per serving)

Calories: 221 / Total fat: 6 grams / Saturated fat: 3 grams / Sodium: 33 mg
Carbohydrate: 41 grams / Fiber: 3 grams / Protein: 3 grams / Cost: $$ / *

Sweet Potato Fries

Prep time: 10 minutes / Cook time: 25 minutes / Makes: 10 servings / Serving size: ¹/₁₀ mixture

What you'll need

5 large sweet potatoes, cut into thin slices

¼ cup canola oil

1 tablespoon onion powder

1 tablespoon garlic powder

1 teaspoon black pepper

Dash salt

1 tablespoon sugar

½ teaspoon cayenne pepper

What to do

1. Preheat oven to 375 degrees.

2. Place potatoes, oil, onion powder, garlic powder, pepper, and salt in large bowl; stir well to combine.

3. Place coated potatoes on large foil-lined cookie sheet coated with cooking spray.

4. Place in oven for 25 minutes or until potatoes are done to desired crispness.

5. In small bowl, blend sugar and cayenne pepper; dust mixture over cooked fries, if desired.

Nutrition facts
(per serving)

Calories: 114

Total fat: 6 grams

Saturated fat: 1 gram

Sodium: 46 mg

Carbohydrate: 15 grams

Fiber: 2 grams

Protein: 1 gram

Cost: $

Sweet Potato Puree with Roasted Bananas, Cinnamon, and Toasted Walnuts

Prep time: 10 minutes / Cook time: 1 hour and 20 minutes / Makes: 10 servings / Serving size: 1/10 mixture

What you'll need

6 large sweet potatoes

2 ripe bananas

6 tablespoons light butter, divided

½ cup pure maple syrup

1 tablespoon ground cinnamon

1 teaspoon ground nutmeg

1 teaspoon ground ginger

½ teaspoon ground cloves

½ teaspoon salt

1 cup walnuts, chopped

1 teaspoon ground cinnamon

2 tablespoons dark brown sugar

What to do

1. Preheat oven to 425 degrees.

2. Place sweet potatoes on cookie sheet; pierce sweet potatoes with fork and bake for about 1 hour or until tender.

3. Roast bananas with skins on for 15 minutes. When cool enough to handle, peel potatoes and bananas and place in food processor.

4. Blend potatoes and bananas until smooth. Add 3 tablespoons light butter, maple syrup, cinnamon, nutmeg, ginger, cloves, and salt. Puree to combine.

5. Place mixture in 9x13-inch glass baking dish coated with cooking spray.

6. In skillet warmed to medium heat, add remaining 3 tablespoons light butter. Add walnuts and sauté until well coated. Sprinkle with cinnamon.

7. Arrange walnuts on top of sweet potato mixture. Sprinkle with brown sugar.

8. Bake at 350 degrees for about 20 minutes.

Nutrition facts (per serving)

Calories: 228 / Total fat: 9 grams / Saturated fat: 2 grams / Sodium: 163 mg
Fiber: 5 grams / Protein: 3 grams / Cost: $ / *

Tangy Poppy Seed Fruit Salad

Prep time: 15 minutes / Makes: 8 servings / Serving size: ½ cup

What you'll need

2 cups fresh pineapple, chopped

2 oranges, peeled and segmented

1 cup seedless grapes

3 kiwi, peeled, halved, and sliced

1 mango, chopped

1 cup strawberries, quartered

1 tablespoon grated lime zest

3 tablespoons lime juice

1 tablespoon honey

1 teaspoon poppy seeds

What to do

1. In large bowl, toss first 6 ingredients.

2. In small bowl, combine zest, juice, honey, and poppy seeds.

3. Stir well and toss with fruit.

Nutrition facts (per serving)

Calories: 100 / Total fat: 1 gram / Saturated fat: 0 grams / Sodium: 3 mg
Carbohydrate: 26 grams / Fiber: 3 grams / Protein: 1 gram / Cost: $

Creator God, thank You for providing us with an abundance

of healthy and delicious food. Amen.

Thai Spicy Yams with Coconut

Prep time: 15 minutes / Cook time: 20 minutes / Makes: 12 servings / Serving size: ¹/₁₂ mixture

What you'll need

3 tablespoons extra-virgin olive oil

2 large red onions, chopped

1 tablespoon garlic, minced

1 tablespoon yellow mustard seeds

2 teaspoons ground cumin

1 teaspoon ground coriander

1 teaspoon salt

1 teaspoon ground turmeric

¼ cup dark brown sugar

5 pounds yams, peeled, cooked, and cut into 1½-inch cubes

½ cup shredded unsweetened coconut

What to do

1. Preheat oven to 400 degrees.

2. Place large skillet over medium-high heat and add oil. Reduce heat to medium and cook onions for about 3 minutes. Add garlic and mustard seeds. Stir until fragrant, about 1 minute.

3. Add cumin, coriander, salt, and turmeric; sauté for another minute.

4. Place yams in large bowl. Pour onion mixture on top along with brown sugar and coconut.

5. Bake in preheated oven for 20 minutes.

Nutrition facts
(per serving)

Calories: 346

Total fat: 10 grams

Saturated fat: 6 grams

Sodium: 23 mg

Carbohydrate: 62 grams

Fiber: 10 grams

Protein: 4 grams

Cost: $$

Waldorf Salad

Prep time: 10 minutes / Chill time: 30 minutes / Makes: 6 servings / Serving size: ½ cup

What you'll need

Salad:

2 cups apples, chopped

1 tablespoon fresh lemon juice

⅓ cup celery, chopped

¼ cup raisins

¼ cup walnuts, chopped

Dressing:

⅓ cup fat-free vanilla yogurt

¼ cup light whipped topping

1 teaspoon grated lemon rind

Dash cinnamon

What to do

1. Place apples in medium mixing bowl. Top with lemon juice and toss. Add celery, raisins, and walnuts; set aside.

2. Mix dressing ingredients together.

3. Add dressing to apple mixture.

4. Chill for 30 minutes.

Nutrition facts (per serving)

Calories: 94 / Total fat: 4 grams / Saturated fat: 1 gram / Sodium: 75 mg
Carbohydrate: 17 grams / Fiber: 1 gram / Protein: 2 grams / Cost: $

White Bean Salad with Grilled Figs

Prep time: 30 minutes / Cook time: 5 minutes / Makes: 6 servings / Serving size: 1 cup

What you'll need

1 (15 ounce) can of cannellini (or navy) beans

¼ red onion, chopped

1 clove of garlic, sliced

2 plum tomatoes, diced

½ lemon, juiced

3 tablespoons olive oil, divided

6 figs, halved

Salt and pepper to taste

¼ cup low-fat feta cheese

1 teaspoon parsley leaves, chopped

½ teaspoon thyme leaves, chopped

What to do

1. Preheat grill.

2. In large bowl, combine beans, onion, garlic, tomatoes, lemon juice, and 2 tablespoons of olive oil. Cover with plastic wrap and chill.

3. Place figs in small bowl and add salt and pepper to taste; drizzle with remaining 1 tablespoon olive oil and toss.

4. Arrange figs on hot grill and cook until charred, 1 to 2 minutes.

5. Remove bowl of beans from refrigerator; add feta cheese, parsley, thyme, and figs. Toss and serve.

Nutrition facts
(per serving)

Calories: 220

Total fat: 9 grams

Saturated fat: 2 grams

Sodium: 464 mg

Carbohydrate: 30 grams

Fiber: 6 grams

Protein: 8 grams

Cost: $$

White Cheddar Herbed Grit Cake over Mixed Greens with Honey-Fig Vinaigrette

Prep time: 10 minutes / Chill time: 1 hour / Cook time: 8 minutes / Makes: 10 salads / Serving size: 1 salad

What you'll need

Vinaigrette:
2 tablespoons honey
4 fresh figs
¼ cup white wine vinegar
3 tablespoons extra-virgin
   olive oil
2 tablespoons water
⅛ teaspoon ground cayenne
   pepper
Sea salt and ground black
   pepper to taste

Grit Cake:
2 cups water
1 cup grits
1 teaspoon onion powder
1 teaspoon garlic powder
1 teaspoon dried basil
1 teaspoon dried oregano
½ teaspoon dried thyme
Sea salt and ground black
   pepper to taste
½ cup white cheddar cheese,
   shredded
2 tablespoons olive oil

Salad:
10 cups spring mix greens
1 cup strawberries, sliced
20 pecan halves, chopped
¼ cup shredded Parmesan
   cheese

What to do

1. For vinaigrette: Combine all ingredients in food processor. Blend until smooth, adding more oil or water until desired consistency is reached. Place vinaigrette in bowl; cover and refrigerate at least an hour.
2. For grit cake: Warm medium saucepan over high heat. Add 2 cups water and bring to boil. Add grits; cover, stirring occasionally until grits are tender, about 6 minutes. Add onion powder, garlic powder, basil, oregano, thyme, salt, and pepper. Cook an additional 5 minutes, stirring occasionally to prevent grits from sticking to saucepan.
3. Place grits in medium mixing bowl and add shredded cheese; stir well. Place mixture in 8x8-inch glass baking dish and refrigerate until firm, about 2 hours. Form mixture into 10 patties. Warm large, nonstick skillet to medium high and add 2 tablespoons olive oil. When skillet is heated, place grit cakes on skillet, cooking about 3 minutes on each side or until golden brown. Place grit cakes on paper towels and keep warm until ready to serve.
4. For salad, pour vinaigrette over salad greens. Divide greens evenly over 10 plates. Garnish plates with sliced strawberries and chopped pecans. Place grit cake in center of each salad and top with shredded Parmesan cheese.

Nutrition facts (per serving)

Calories: 191 / Total fat: 12 grams / Saturated fat: 3 grams / Sodium: 228 mg
Carbohydrate: 19 grams / Fiber: 2 grams / Protein: 5 grams / Cost: $$$

Wild Rice Pilaf

Prep time: 20 minutes / Cook time: 15 minutes / Makes: 16 servings / Serving size: ½ cup

What you'll need

3 tablespoons olive oil

1 cup onion, chopped

2 cups mushrooms, chopped

3 cloves garlic, chopped

3 cups cooked brown rice

3 cups cooked wild rice

½ cup green onions,
   sliced thin

Salt and pepper to taste

- -

What to do

1. Warm oil in large sauté pan over medium heat; add onion, mushrooms, and garlic and simmer for 12 minutes.

2. Add remaining ingredients. Stir well and cook until rice is thoroughly heated, about 3 minutes.

3. Serve warm.

Nutrition facts
(per serving)

Calories: 102

Total fat: 3 grams

Saturated fat: 0 grams

Sodium: 4 mg (without salt)

Carbohydrate: 17 grams

Fiber: 2 grams

Protein: 3 grams

Cost: $

Special thanks to our cookbook testers:

The Church Health Center Wellness Education Staff:
Mary Cay Oyler, Sharon Tagg, Marissa Harris, Robin Rutherford, Carissa Algea, Carolyn Nichols, Suzanne Ray, Sheila Harrell, Brooke Beck, Laura Todd, Esther Wills, Jane Donnelly

Church Health Center Staff:
Mike Sturdivant, Jenny Bartlett-Prescott, Lisa Carson, Linda Nelson, Susan McGee, Patty Newsom, Denise Hensley, Susan Chick, Emily Young, Patrice Griffin, Zamrya Lambert, Ann Marie Barber, Rachael Thompson, Alison Tucker, Stacy Smith, Ann Langston, Mary Gilleland

Community Testers:
Beth Boyle, Rosie Wedaman, Edna Pakkala, Rita Hilgenhold, Cecilia Clanton, Kay Rutherford, Ruth Taylor, Virginia Stanley, Peter Kesser, Elsie Yeates, Andrus Clayton, Sam Miller, Ann Erickson, Cathy Alexander, Carole Hooper, Joseph Dowsley, Leslie Bouldin, Susan Mealer, Barbara Weaver, Emily Turner, Barbara Riley, Leslie Bouldin, Kim Mitchell, Judy LaRiviere, Cynthia Shambaugh, Meg McGill, Janet Claxton, Alice McGaughey, Kitrina Poe, Pat McFarland, Jane Antrobus, Reba Roberts, Caroline MacQueen, Cynthia Burnette, Mike Walczyk, Betsy Hutchins, John Gasquet, Bianca Burks, Amy Duesterhaus, Barbara Strong, Linda Young, Maggie Beason, Edna Pakkala, Elsie Yeates, Rosie Wedaman, Marilyn Young, Elizabeth Gigger, Jane Donnelly

Thanks to the staff and friends of the Church Health Center who contributed prayers to this book:

DeeDee Brinkman, Lisa Carson, Stephanie Cherry-Hurd, Maureen Daniels, Jennie Dickerson, Lizy Heard, Susan Hanifl, Johnnie Hatten, Ollie Johnson, Kara Kilpatrick, Debra Livingston, Linda Nelson, Patti Newsom, Butch Odom, Geraldine Pollard, T'Challa Pollard, Carol Redden, Philinese Seals, Stacy Smith, Sharon Tagg

Index